The Bible in the Middle Ages:
Its Influence on Literature and Art

medieval & renaissance texts & studies

VOLUME 89

The Bible in the Middle Ages:
Its Influence on Literature and Art

Edited by

BERNARD S. LEVY

Medieval & Renaissance texts & studies
Binghamton, New York
1992

Library of Congress Cataloging-in-Publication Data

The Bible in the Middle Ages : its influence on literature and art
/ edited by Bernard S. Levy

    p. cm. — (Medieval & Renaissance texts & studies ; v. 89)
    "Six essays . . originally read during the plenary sessions of the
Nineteenth Annual Conference sponsored by the Center for Medieval
and Early Renaissance Studies of the State University of New York at
Binghamton held on October 18–19, 1985"—Pref.
    Includes bibliographical references and index.
    ISBN 0–86698–101–2
    1. Bible—Influence—Civilization, Medieval—Congresses.
2. Bible—Criticism, interpretation, etc.—History—Middle Ages, 600–
1500—Congresses. I. Levy, Bernard S., 1927– . II. Title. III. Series.
BS538.7.B57 1992
220'.09'02—dc20   91–34263
                                                         CIP

Contents

Preface

Bernard S. Levy

The six essays contained in the present volume were originally read during the plenary sessions of the Nineteenth
Annual Conference sponsored by the Center for Medieval and
Early Renaissance Studies of the State University of New York
at Binghamton held on October 18–19, 1985. The papers demonstrate the range both in subject matter and in time of the
rather large topic of the conference—"The Bible in the Middle
Ages: Its Influence on Literature and Art"—spanning the period
from the very beginning to the very end of the era and encom-
passing such diverse topics as biblical exegesis, hagiography,
literary uses of the Bible, images of prophecy, illuminations in
manuscripts, stained glass windows, wall painting, and sculpture. A wide variety of writers also are discussed, including, for
example, Augustine, Bonaventure, Andreas Capellanus, Dante,
Chrétien de Troyes, and Christine de Pizan. The volume thus
provides both a very good general introduction and individual
essays that explore specific aspects of this very large topic,
where even a small detail can serve to illuminate the subject.
The volume thus offers something for both the specialist, who
will be rewarded by reading an individual essay, and the
general student of the Bible or of the Middle Ages, who will
find great riches in both the individual essays and the volume
as a whole.

In his essay on "The Scriptural Self," John Alford analyzes
the process of the "transformation of scriptural models into

scriptural selves" by considering "the models," "the logic of transformation," and "the living results." He traces the idea of the Bible as a "pattern book" from St. Paul, who not only advises his audience to be imitators of Christ but also suggests that they can imitate him as an imitator of Christ, thus presenting a pattern of such imitation that can be passed on. Alford suggests that St. Paul's view provided the basis for the saint's life, since "the saints are, by definition, *copies* of Christ, or other biblical heroes, brought up to date." Alford analyzes the *Life of St. Francis* as a prime example in which Bonaventure emphasizes the ways in which Francis imitated Christ in his life and suppresses those aspects of his character that did not reflect such imitation. He also shows that the events in the saints' lives are presented in such a way as to give typological significance by frequent reference to biblical heroes and villains. In order to show how the transformation takes place, Alford analyzes two different views: the first in terms of the image of the mirror, *speculum*, posited on the idea that God's word was a mirror, in which the viewer could see not only his "present self but also his potential self," and thus achieve transformation through an active "engagement of the will"; the second in terms of St. Paul's exhortation "Be ye imitators of me," developed by an interpretation of Genesis 30, "the story of Jacob's genetic experiments with the sheep and goats of his father-in-law, Laban," suggesting an "almost subconscious process." Alford then argues that, because many medieval people considered the biblical patterns important in their lives, it was common in saints' lives to "*arrange* a life after the fact" so that it conformed to the scriptural model.

In a wide-ranging essay on "The Bible as Thesaurus for Secular Literature," Joan M. Ferrante focuses on "the a-religious, irreligious, or anti-religious (at least anti-clerical) use of the Bible in secular literature." She demonstrates the great variety of ways that medieval authors appropriated the Bible for their own distinctive purposes: to make political statements, to enhance love stories, to support pleas for money, to criticize clerical defects. For example, she demonstrates the diversity in the use of biblical allusion in the pursuit of love by citing authors as different as Andreas Capellanus, who has the men in

his dialogues use biblical citations to try to persuade women to
respond to their advances and has the women use the Bible to
dissuade them; Dante, who in his *Vita Nuova* presents Beatrice
as "a Christ figure" who "draws him back to God"; Gottfried
von Strassburg, who uses biblical imagery to present his hero
Tristan as a champion of God by associating him in his early
life with David and to suggest that the existence of the adulterous lovers in the Minnegrotte is parallel to the Garden of Eden
before the fall; and Chrétien de Troyes, who associates Christ's
death and resurrection with an adulterous woman and an
adulterous knight—Ferrante finds this last example "unsettling," even though the purpose of such imagery is to demonstrate that courtly love is idolatrous. She contrasts Dante, who
associates himself with Christ so that his audience will accept
him as a "spokesman of God," and the Archipoeta and Ruggiero Apugliese as authors who, in order to make pleas on their
own behalf, associate themselves with Christ for selfish reasons.
She concludes with a discussion of the use of the Bible for
attacks on clerical corruption, citing works as diverse as the
Roman de la Rose, in which Genius, who is both "Nature's priest
and a priest of the church," dressed as a bishop, "addresses
Love's army, promising them paradise if they do love's work,
as if they were going on a crusade, instead of a rape"; Dante
and Walter of Chatillon, who use the Bible for direct attacks on
clerical corruption; and the "gospel according to Saint Silver
Mark," which she considers the "most impressive example of
preaching the Bible against clerics."

In his carefully reasoned and closely argued essay on "Images of Prophecy: The Old Testament and Medieval Narrative,"
Stephen G. Nichols focuses "on the language theories of the
Fathers, on their study of the *material* aspects of biblical discourse." He first discusses Augustine's *De Doctrina Christiana;*
here Augustine presents a theory of reading in which the reader
will not read the text in and for itself, but will "imitate a doctrinally orthodox reading theory" in which the signs in the text
are "signs for other things." He then discusses Augustine's
view of the language of the prophets. He suggests that since in
the Hebrew Bible prophecy was considered "a gift, a demonstration of the *divine* and the *human* acting directly in history,"

the "prophetic consciousness . . . affirmed the proximity of the divine and the human, rather than the distance between the two." The point here, according to Nichols, is that "the Old Testament viewpoint stresses the materiality of language," in which the prophet "engages in a dialogue" with God, which, "at least rhetorically, postulates a fellowship or equality of speakers"; in this fellowship each understands the other "by direct apprehension of the other's speech," not "by intellectual processes, such as analogy, metaphor, or induction, but directly." Nichols suggests that this view of Old Testament textuality could be a threat to the "Augustinian conception of the word" since, though it "might encourage *commentary*," it would discourage "exegesis in the sense developed by Augustine." After analyzing two incidents from Ezekiel involving "corporeal discourse" to illustrate prophetic discourse, he discusses Augustine's opposition to the "powerful image of the word which links society and history via the person of the prophet" by the substitution of "a new conventional system of signs that stress intellectual engagement over the personal, elective, and emotional modes of intuition that mark Ezekiel's language so strongly." For Augustine, Nichols suggests, the intellectual processes are thus to be controlled by the pedagogue, who stands "between the audience and the phenomenon to be understood." Nichols then discusses hagiography "as a dramatic example of the pedagogical anthropology inaugurated by Augustine" and offers an analysis of the eleventh-century *Vie de saint Alexis* to illustrate his view. He thus concludes, "The power of the saint . . . lies in its potency to continue to demonstrate, recapitulatively, the dominance of the patristic paradigm over the prophetic consciousness." Nichols then discusses the *Alexis* as a work that not only looks back to the Augustinian model of Christian intellectualism but also looks forward "to what Brian Stock has recently described as a new socialization of knowledge" in which "the twelfth-century intellectual did not *embody a subject personally*: he taught it. Being an intellectual was a profession, even a social role." He suggests that this change allowed a more objective view of the Old Testament, as seen in Hugh of St. Victor, who emphasizes the letter of the Old Testament, so that in Hugh and his successors "the concept of allegorical interpretation" was "replaced by the analogical method of exegesis." He argues that in contrast to allegory, which "denies or suppresses the difference of the original text," analogy "allows both elements in a comparison to retain their properties of difference while permitting the evocation of their similarities." He then concludes, "Applied to the question of prophetic identity in the late Middle Ages, the new system of analogical exegesis moves away from the concept of the saint to envisage a new kind of Christian prophet who fulfills an analogous social, historical, and theological role to that of the Old Testament prophet." Nichols concludes his essay with a demonstration of how the new system of analogical exegesis works by a careful and remarkable examination of Christine de Pizan's "fascinating and largely misunderstood work," the _Ditié de Jehanne d'Arc_.

In his essay on "Pictorial Emphases in Early Biblical Manuscripts," Robert G. Calkins discusses what he considers an important but neglected "avenue of analysis, intrinsic to the nature of the book": "the creation of a programmatic statement achieved through either decorative or pictorial emphasis." Before focusing on the achievement of such a programmatic statement in the Lambeth Bible in London, Calkins explores earlier biblical manuscripts in order to discover "the background of choices from which such emphasis was derived." He discusses and traces two parallel traditions of illustration, one involving a "copiously expanded narrative pictorial tradition," the other, "the use of a single miniature to introduce a volume, individual books of the Bible, or groups of books, usually a frontispiece." He suggests that "the latter tradition is a synoptic mode of illustration" that "makes possible a didactic or programmatic selection or juxtaposition of images that go beyond a mere narrative function." Since, as he notes, it was difficult to provide pictorial amplification in a one-volume Bible, various alternatives were developed. Following a discussion of such alternatives, he concludes that "the illumination of major English Romanesque Bibles" evolved from the "tradition of introductory embellishment for each book of the Bible and its preface." He then focuses on two major Romanesque Bibles, the Bury and Lambeth Bibles, arguing that in these, "patterns of emphasis ... emerge by means of concentrations of historiated initials and miniatures interspersed at only selected points among the standard fare of decorative initials." In the Bury Bible he discovers an "emphasis on the early historical books— the *ante* and *sub lege*, the linking of the Law and the prophesies through the story of the birth of Samuel ... and on the four major prophets." Calkins further notes that the distribution of historiated initials and pictorial frontispieces of the Old Testament volumes of these Bibles reveals that there is a heavy pictorial emphasis on the Books of the Prophets and, in the Lambeth Bible, on the Book of Daniel. Calkins argues that the particular choice of miniatures in these Bibles did not depend "merely on the availability of certain pictorial models," but reflected a wider concern in the Romanesque period with the prophets as primary spokesmen in the Church's struggle against heretical movements, Jews, and infidels. Calkins further suggests that the extraordinary weight given to the prophet Daniel in the Lambeth Bible reflects a burgeoning interest in Daniel as a particularly appropriate spokesman for these concerns, which he finds reflected in the liturgical emphasis on readings from Daniel and other prophets, on the use of the *Sermon against the Jews, Pagans and Arians Concerning the Creed* of the Pseudo-Augustine, and on the para-liturgical plays of the *Ordo Prophetarum* and the Play of Daniel, all of which, he suggests, were read or performed during the Advent-Christmas season in twelfth-century England. Calkins concludes that, though "we cannot speak of a specific, focused program" in the selection of miniatures in the Bury and Lambeth Bibles, we can see that they reflect "a deliberate choice to articulate those books of the Bible that carried the message most appropriate for the concerns of the day."

In her essay "Biblical Stories in Windows: Were They Bibles for the Poor?" Madeline H. Caviness questions an idea that appears to have had support from both modern and medieval writers, arguing that it must be modified, since if there were such teaching, it would have been for the illiterate, regardless of class, rather than for the poor as such. She brings the question to light by a careful examination of narrative sequences corresponding to biblical stories in stained glass windows from the

second half of the twelfth through the mid-thirteenth century (a
form of monumental art "often accessible to the public," in
monastic churches, cathedrals, and a palace chapel), in order to
discover the positions given to biblical subjects, the way they
were treated (narrative, typological, symbolic), and the source
texts. In her survey she is concerned with the extent to which
Bible stories of various sorts used in the windows of the period
formed a normative pattern for the period, and she considers
several kinds of biblical windows containing different subjects
in order to discover what could be learned about "programs"
and "favorite subjects." She suggests that the programs in the
monastic churches could not have been Bibles for the poor,
because, since they were designed for the edification of monks,
their subjects were too esoteric to be useful for such a purpose.
She does discover, however, that there are isolated biblical
stories in the cathedrals that were very popular, including the
parables and histories of Old Testament heroes, such as Noah
and Joseph. In the course of her discussion, Caviness considers
the various possible ways that windows could be "read" and
discovers that they could not really be "read" by the illiterate,
because, for example, "windows do not usually read like pages
of a book," and that "the narratives most often expand upon
the events described in the Vulgate." She then studies several
representations of the most popular story, the Joseph cycle, to
discover what such an examination can contribute to the question posed, offering critical analysis of the presentations along
the way. What she finds is that the windows presenting the
Joseph story emphasize different aspects of the story ("no two
are alike"), based on versions of the story expanded beyond
that presented in the Old Testament, and suggest a great variety
of interpretations, depending on such matters as the context in
which it is portrayed and the patronage. Joseph could, Caviness
demonstrates, be a figure for Christ, the priesthood, a faithful
steward, "a younger son in a feudal society that was in the
process . . . of adapting to patrilineage," a freed man, a visionary, or an overseer. Caviness then argues that since in the
period surveyed "texts and pictures have equal autonomy,"
"windows (since they are public) are as likely to have influenced texts as the other way." Since the biblical windows that

she has studied do not teach the Bible to the illiterate, but present moralized stories and provide role models, Caviness thus concludes: "I tend to see these windows indeed as Bibles of the laity, but it is a Bible transformed into popular romance, more vividly reflecting contemporary structures than esoteric spiritual truths."

In his study of "Old Testament Illustration in Thirteenth-Century England," Nigel Morgan examines the Old Testament subjects chosen for illustration in both manuscript illumination and monumental cycles in wall painting and sculpture. He argues that biblical paraphrases, such as the *Historica Scholastica* of Petrus Comestor, the *Aurora* of Peter Riga, the *Compendium historiae in genealogia Christi* of Peter of Poitiers and the "vernacular paraphrases" which depended upon them, such as the "Bible" of Herman of Valenciennes, the Middle English *Genesis and Exodus, Iacop and Iosef,* and *Cursor Mundi,* became "fundamental reference books for the rest of the Middle Ages" and clearly influenced the choice of subject in cycles of pictures found in the prefatory miniatures of Psalters as well as in monumental wall painting and sculpture. In his discussion he considers the likelihood of an intermediary such as a clerical advisor acting on behalf of a patron having knowledge of the biblical paraphrases. He suggests that the different emphases in each cycle may have resulted from the varied relationships between patron, advisor, and artist. He further proposes, however, that even in those cases where the choice of stories was a result of patronage, the influence of the biblical paraphrases is evident in the "exact choice of scenes within these stories" and "in the way in which the story was told." Morgan then demonstrates the validity of his thesis concerning the influence of the Latin and vernacular biblical paraphrases by analyzing the "extra-biblical" scenes, the order of the scenes, and the use of rare scenes in the cycles from the lives of Adam and Eve, Cain, and Joseph. He concludes that the "choice and selection of subject matter" in the thirteenth-century cycles "in many cases is more closely paralleled in the emphases of the paraphrases than that in the Vulgate itself, and that these texts, and individual preferences of the patron or clerical advisor, were the determining element of the content of the pictorial cycle."

Although each of the essays in this volume can profitably be read for its own intrinsic value, readers will find that there are important threads that weave their way through the volume and thus tie the various essays together. Two of the literary essays deal extensively with saints' lives from quite different perspectives, but there are some important ideas that inspire both essays. For example, both Alford and Nichols suggest that the hagiographer arranges the deeds of his subject after the fact to conform to a pattern, discuss the Old Testament patriarchs referred to in saints' lives as types of Christ, note the pattern of a life of a saint as an _imitatio Christi_, and indicate that the purpose of the life of the saint was to instruct and to edify by presenting an example to be imitated. Ferrante, on the other hand, focuses on the use of the Bible by secular writers for non-religious purposes and explores the great variety of ways that they make use of biblical allusions; she thus does not examine saints' lives. She is, however, as are Alford and Nichols, interested in the Bible as a source of exemplars for medieval writers. She suggests that, although the secular writers often present the biblical exemplars in the traditional roles, they also present them in less traditional roles—for example, Solomon in his customary role as source of wisdom but also as the deceived lover—using the exemplars for their own special purposes. Just as the literary essays, though written independently, show connections with one another, so too do the essays dealing with medieval art. In fact, each of the three art historians notes that the selection of biblical subjects that are illustrated is determined at least in part by the ways in which they can be used to reflect contemporary concerns. Specifically, Calkins suggests that a pictorial emphasis on the book of Daniel and the other major prophets in the illustrated Bibles that he examines reflects concerns of later Romanesque dogma and art with threats to orthodoxy, both from heresy and from Jews rejecting Christ as the Savior; and Caviness, discussing an apocryphal scene from the Joseph cycle in a stained glass window at Chartres, suggests that in the judgment scene depicted damnation may be emphasized over salvation because of the "trials of heretics and the increasing pressure on the Jews to convert to Christianity in the early thirteenth century." Caviness, studying stained glass windows, and Morgan, focusing on illustrated manuscripts and wall paintings, both deal at some length with Joseph cycles, and both make reference to vernacular paraphrases of the Bible. However, while Morgan argues that these biblical paraphrases had an important influence on the choice and selection of subject matter in the pictorial cycles he examines, Caviness suggests that "windows (since they are public) are as likely to have influenced vernacular texts as the other way around." In their conclusions, there is also a striking similarity: Caviness comments, "I tend to see these windows as Bibles of the laity, but it is a Bible transformed into popular romance, more vividly reflecting sociological structures than esoteric spiritual truths"; and Morgan concludes, "To many people the stories of the Old Testament were familiar, but both in pictures and texts they had been adapted in ways such that they resembled more the romances of contemporary writers, and thus presented narrative contexts appropriate to the tastes and issues of the times." These comments, of course, connect the essays with the analyses of Ferrante, who, among other things, discusses the uses of the Bible in several medieval romances. Readers will find many threads that bind the essays dealing with art and those dealing with literature, but they will also find that there are many common concerns in all of the essays that help to unify the volume in ways that go beyond the basic concern with the various ways that the Bible influenced literature and art in the Middle Ages and thus make it worthwhile for the reader, no matter what his or her interest may be in a specific essay, to read the volume as a whole.

I wish to thank several people who made the Conference and this volume possible: Paul E. Szarmach, Director of the Center for Medieval and Renaissance Studies (CEMERS), for his support and encouragement; Dorothy Huber, then Secretary of the Center, who helped to organize many of the details of the Conference; Mario A. Di Cesare, Director of Medieval & Renaissance Texts & Studies (MRTS), for his support and encouragement; Michael Pavese, Senior Editor of MRTS, who guided the volume through the process of publication; and Helene Scheck, who prepared the index for the volume. Because of the exigencies of the publication process, it was not possible to offer as full a volume of the conference papers as I would have liked. I am grateful to those who presented papers in the many sessions of the Conference, and I regret that those papers could not be published. I particularly regret that I was unable to include "The Bible as Image in the Middle Ages," a paper presented by Milton McC. Gatch. Professor Gatch came to the rescue of the program at a time when it looked as if the concept for the conference would dissolve. I appreciate his collegial generosity and deeply regret that it was not possible to publish his paper in the volume. Finally, I wish to thank the contributors, for without their patience and cooperation during the long process of publication, there would be no volume.

The Scriptural Self

John A. Alford

S t. Bonaventure, reflecting the medieval tendency to Platonic exemplarism, writes in his *Collations*, "Being can exist in only two ways: either as subsistent, self-modeled, and self-intended; or as contingent, modeled on another, and tending to another."[1] Of the two categories of being, only God is subsistent; all else is contingent. Since we are modeled after God, Bonaventure would argue, we achieve our perfection only as we tend toward Him. To conform to his image in us is to realize our own true selves.

Conversely, it follows that we deny our true selves when we wilfully pursue nonconformity or (to use the expressive Middle English term) *singularity*. Like the devil, according to *The Book of Vices and Virtues*, the person who abandons the divine model, who "weneþ or tristeþ more to hymself þan he scholde," is guilty of "syngulertee, þat is onlyhede": "For þe proude and þe surquidous man, þat weneþ to kunne more or be of more my3t or be worþier þan oþere, ne wole not don as oþere doþ þat ben bettere þan he, but wole be soleyn, þat is only, in his doynges."[2] The author of *Piers Plowman* describes one of his most

---

For several bibliographical items in the notes below, I am grateful to an anonymous reader for the press.

[1] *The Works of Bonaventure*, trans. José de Vinck (Paterson, NJ, 1970), 5:7.

[2] Ed. W. Nelson Francis, EETS 217 (London, 1942; repr. 1968), 17.

vivid creations, Haukyn the active man, as "so singuler by him-self . . . Was noon swich as hymself . . . an ordre by hymselue."[3] And near the end of the fifteenth century, Wynkyn de Worde speaks of the misery that comes with the delusion that we can be self-modeled: "Through sin the soul drowneth in despair / Then sitteth the soul from solace, singulayre / On every side with sorrow umbesette."[4] In short, to conform to a pattern is to be somebody. Not to conform is to be nobody. Those who desire to be different, singular, an order unto themselves, are less likely to assert their identity than to lose it altogether.

Within this frame of thought, the Bible occupies a central place in the Middle Ages. It is the great storehouse of exemplars. It is a record of the historical manifestations of divine Being in the lives of numerous men and women, lives that may serve as patterns of identity. It is utterly complete. No pattern of virtue or right living has been omitted. Bonaventure says: "If you seek an example of patience, behold Job and Tobias; of magnanimity, behold David fighting Goliath, and Judas Mac-chabee; of faith, behold Abraham and the glorious Virgin," and so forth.[5] Bonaventure believed, as did many of his contemporaries, that outside the Bible there was no pattern of life worth living. In the words of St. Gregory, "Scripture tells the deeds of the saints and excites the hearts of the weak to imitate them. . . . We ought to transform what we read into our very selves."[6]

This transformation of scriptural models into scriptural selves is my subject. I would like to analyze the process in three

---

[3] *Piers Plowman: The B Version*, ed. George Kane and E. Talbot Don-aldson (London, 1975), 13.282–84. Subsequent quotations are from this edition. Quotations from the C version are from Derek Pearsall's edition (Berkeley, 1978). In citing the passage ("singular" III.9: "Separate from others by reason of superiority or pre-eminence"), the OED misses entirely the negative connotations of the word.

[4] *Contemplacioun of Synnes* (Westminster: Wynken de Worde, 1499), sig. F, p. v.

[5] *Works of Bonaventure*, 5:256.

[6] *Moralia in Iob*, PL 75:542C, quoted in Jerome Taylor, trans., *The Didascalicon of Hugh of St. Victor* (New York, 1961), 220.

stages, considering first the models, then the logic of transformation, and finally the living results.

I

The idea of the Bible as a pattern book is itself biblical. Its main
exponent is St. Paul. In both 1 Cor. 4.16 and 1 Cor. 11.1, he
writes, "Be ye imitators of me, as I also am of Christ."[7] Because
he is an imitator of Christ, his own life in turn is worthy of
imitation. He sees the process as a chain reaction. In 1 Thess.
1.6–7, he reminds his spiritual children, "And you became
imitators of us and of the Lord ... so that you were made a
pattern to all that believe in Macedonia and Achaia." So Christ
was a pattern for Paul, Paul for the Thessalonians, and the
Thessalonians for their countrymen in general. The thinking is
genetic. The image of Christ is reincarnated, continually renewed, passed from one spiritual generation to the next.

In this brief sketch of Pauline exemplarism, we see the rationale for a whole literary genre—the saint's life. The replication of
Christ's image in Paul, and then in the church at Thessalonika,
and then throughout Macedonia, is continued in an unbroken
succession of holy biographies. The same patterns recur over
and over. For the saints are, by definition, *copies* of Christ or of
other biblical heroes, brought up to date. The whole nature of
the genre is summarized in one of its most characteristic words:
another. The young St. Aelred is "another Daniel"; St. Gilbert of
Sempringham, "another Job"; St. Francis, "well-nigh another
Christ."[8]

Bonaventure's *Life of St. Francis* presents an especially well-
documented case of scriptural modeling.[9] The central theme is

---

[7] All biblical citations are from the Douai version.

[8] *The Life of Aelred of Rievaulx, by Walter Daniel*, trans. F. M. Powicke
(London, 1950), 9; *John Capgrave's Lives of St. Augustine and St. Gilbert of
Sempringham and a Sermon*, ed. J. J. Munro, EETS 140 (London, 1910), 95;
*"The Little Flowers" and the Life of St. Francis with the "Mirror of Perfec-
tion"*, introduction by T. Okey (London, 1910), 14.

[9] Trans. in *"The Little Flowers" and the Life of St. Francis*, 303–97.
Subsequent quotations are from this text.

stated as follows: "The grace of God our Saviour hath in these latter days appeared in His servant Francis . . . , set as an example unto them that do perfectly follow after Christ" (303–4). Throughout the biography Bonaventure takes great pains to point out the many ways in which Francis fulfilled the pattern of holy life. For example, Francis imitated the pattern of the apostolic life to the letter—no money, scrip, shoes, staff, or second coat. When he sought papal sanction for his _Rule_, the argument that moved Innocent III was that Francis was seeking to imitate "the pattern of Gospel life" (320). And against the widespread criticism that Francis's public displays of humility were excessive, Bonaventure defends the saint with the argument that, "Yet . . . it set forth a pattern of perfect humility, whereby the follower of Christ was taught . . ." (337), thus echoing Paul's own defense of his gratuitous behavior in 2 Thess. 3.9: "For it is not as if we had not the power [to do otherwise] but that we might give ourselves a pattern unto you, to imitate us." The pattern is everything. From start to finish Bonaventure emphasizes the numerous parallels between Francis and Christ, culminating, of course, in the receiving of the stigmata, whereby Francis was "wholly transformed into the likeness of Christ crucified" (385). The saint's eccentricities or merely personal attributes—the very things that would bring him alive for the modern reader—are suppressed as insignificant. Clearly, this is not biography in the usual sense of the word. It is a dramatic working out of Bonaventure's own metaphysics: God is self-modeled; all other being, including Francis, is contingent, modeled on another, and tending to another. It was Francis's special merit to have acknowledged this truth totally with his own life.

Not only the saints themselves but also the events of which they are a part tend to show typological significance. Their world is peopled with biblical heroes and villains. Accounts such as the following from Eddius Stephanus's _Life of Bishop Wilfrid_, written in the early eighth century, are not at all unusual.

While they were crossing the British sea on their return from Gaul with Bishop Wilfrid of blessed memory, and the

priests were praising God with psalms and hymns, giving
the time to the oarsmen, a violent storm arose in mid-ocean
and the winds were contrary, *just as they were to the disciples
of Jesus on the sea of Galilee*. The wind blew hard from the
south-east and the foam-crested waves hurled them on to
the land of the South Saxons which they did not know. . . .
Forthwith a huge army of pagans arrived intending to seize
the ship. . . . The holy bishop spoke to them soothingly and
peaceably. . . . The enemy however were fierce, and, *harden-
ing their hearts like Pharaoh*, were unwilling to let the people
of God depart. . . . The chief priest of their idolatrous worship also took up his stand in front of the pagans, on a
high mound, *and like Balaam*, attempted to curse the people
of God. . . . Thereupon one of the companions of our bishop
took a stone which had been blessed by all the people of
God and hurled it from his sling *after the manner of David*.
It pierced the wizard's forehead and penetrated to his brain
as he stood cursing; death took him unawares *as it did
Goliath*, and his lifeless body fell backwards on to the sand.
The pagans then got ready for battle, but in vain did they
draw up their array against the people of God. For the
Lord fought for the few, *even as when Gideon* with his 300
warriors at the bidding of the Lord slew 120,000 Midianite
warriors at one onslaught. *In the same way* these companions of our holy bishop being well-armed and brave in
heart though but few in number (there were 120 of them,
equal in number to the years of the age of Moses), formed a
plan and made a compact that none should turn his back
upon another in flight, but that they would either win
death with honour or life with victory, God being able with
equal ease to bring either event to pass. So St. Wilfrid the
bishop and his clergy on bended knees lifted their hands
again to heaven and gained the help of the Lord. *For as
Moses* continually called upon the Lord for help, Hur and
Aaron raising his hands, *while Joshua* the son of Nun was
fighting against Amalek with the people of God, *so this
little band of Christians* overthrew the fierce and untamed
heathen host, three times putting them to flight with no

little slaughter, though, marvellous to relate, only five of
the Christians were slain.[10]

Under the weight of so many scriptural comparisons—Christ,
Pharaoh, Balaam, David, Goliath, Gideon, Moses, Joshua—the
account can hardly breathe. A modern translator comments,
"The Old Testament images add heroic scope to the narrative,
just as allusions to earlier heroes of epic and saga do to the *Iliad*
and *Beowulf*."[11] This is undoubtedly true, yet I cannot think of
a comparable passage in either of these works. Clearly, the main
purpose of all these biblical allusions is to invoke the central
truth of Old Testament history, namely, that God intervenes to
protect his people who put their trust in him. Whatever does
not fit this pattern—for example, a more detailed account of the
fighting itself, such as one would certainly expect from an epic
or saga—is simply omitted.

Because the pattern of a saint's life is everything, the story
depends almost entirely on deeds. Conversation is rare. William
of Malmesbury makes a very revealing excuse in his *Life of St.
Wulfstan* for failing to report the saint's own words: "I have
omitted to relate the words which were spoken or may have
been spoken from time to time, being anxious in all things not
to jeopardize the truth. It is the mark of an idle man to dispense
words when deeds may suffice."[12]

When saints do speak, the words are not often their own.
Most of them, as Dumontier says of St. Bernard, "talk Bible."[13]
The pastiches that make up their speech function less to reveal
their character than to further define the pattern, to assimilate
them in yet another way to scriptural typology. To this general
rule, there are of course some notable exceptions. One of the
most remarkable features about Eadmer's *Life of Anselm*, as R.

---

[10] *The Life of Bishop Wilfrid by Eddius Stephanus*, ed. and trans. Bertram Colgrave (Cambridge, 1927; repr. 1985), 27–29.

[11] Clinton Albertson, trans., *Anglo-Saxon Saints and Heroes* (Bronx, NY, 1967), 109 n.

[12] R. W. Southern, *St. Anselm and His Biographer* (Cambridge, 1962), 334.

[13] *St. Bernard et la Bible* (Paris, 1953), 17.

W. Southern points out, is the biographer's apparent attempt to report Anselm's actual words.[14]

The anonymous *Life of Christina of Markyate*, composed in the early fourteenth century, presents an especially interesting compromise with convention.[15] To her family and friends, Christina speaks in her own idiom; to God, in his. Let me cite just two contrasting examples. Married against her will by her parents, she asks her new husband for a relationship modeled after that of St. Cecilia and Valerian:

"Let us, therefore," she exhorted him, "follow their example, so that we may become their companions in eternal glory. Because if we suffer with them, we shall also reign with them. Do not take it amiss that I have declined your embraces. In order that your friends may not reproach you with being rejected by me, I will go home with you: and let us live together there for some time, ostensibly as husband and wife, but in reality living chastely in the sight of the Lord. But first let us join hands in a compact that neither meanwhile will touch the other unchastely, neither will look upon the other except with a pure and angelic gaze, making a promise that in three or four years' time we will receive the religious habit and offer ourselves ... to some monastery which providence shall appoint" (51).

Except for the opening conflation of Romans 8.17 and 2 Timothy 2.12, Christina here speaks in her own words. In contrast

---

[14] *St. Anselm and His Biographer*, 333.

[15] *The Life of Christina of Markyate*, ed. and trans. C. H. Talbot (Oxford, 1959), 89–91. Subsequent quotations are from this text. To the literary evidence of Christina's use of models, we may add the visual evidence of the *St. Albans Psalter*, made expressly for Christina, which includes an illustrated Life of St. Alexis intended to serve, apparently, as a paradigm of her own life. As Francis Wormald observes, the scenes chosen for illustration are "the very scenes which were of topical interest in a book destined for Christina, scenes which could be understood as allegories of her own actions"; see Otto Pächt, C. R. Dodwell, and Francis Wormald, *The St. Albans Psalter*, Studies of the Warburg Institute, 25 (London, 1960), 140.

she habitually addresses God in the words of Scripture. Desper-
ate after her husband attempts (with her parents' complicity) to
force himself upon her, she prays as follows:

> O Lord my God, my only hope [cf. Ps. 70.5, 141.6], the
> searcher out of hearts and feelings [cf. Apoc. 2.23], whom
> alone I wish to please, is it Thy pleasure that I should be
> deprived of my wish [cf. Ps. 77.30]? If thou deliver me not
> this day, I shall be left in the world, anxious about worldly
> things and how to please my husband [1 Cor. 7.34]. My
> one desire, as Thou knowest, is to please Thee alone and to
> be united to Thee for all time without end. But whether this
> be Thy decision will become clear if today Thou drive me
> from my father's house and from my relatives [Gen. 24.40],
> nevermore to return. For it is better for me never to leave it
> than to return like a dog to its vomit [Prov. 26.11]. But
> Thou seest what is more profitable for me: I wish not my
> will, but Thine to come to pass for ever [cf. Luke 22.42].
> Blessed be Thy name for evermore [Ps. 71.17] (89–91).

Although Christina's prayer seems to describe her condition
perfectly, it is little more than a cento of biblical quotations.

Theoretically, the representation of saints' speeches would
seem to offer the perfect opportunity for a significant variety of
rhetorical styles. After all, as Alexander Murray has emphasized, saints are by definition "socially amphibious," taking as
their motto Paul's words in 1 Cor. 1.19, "I became all things to
all men, that I might by all means save some."[16] For Eadmer,
St. Anselm embodied this ideal: "For he adapted his words to
every class of men, so that his hearers declared that nothing
could have been spoken more appropriate to their station."[17]
Nevertheless, hagiographers in general are not disposed to
illustrate this ideal in terms of direct discourse. Eadmer may
distinguish between Anselm's private and public utterances (the
latter more steeped in Scripture)[18] and the author of Christina

---

[16] *Reason and Society in the Middle Ages* (Oxford, 1985), 386–401.

[17] *St. Anselm and His Biographer*, 55.

[18] For example, *St. Anselm and His Biographer*, 93–97.

of Markyate's *Life* may represent her as speaking differently to God and man, but most of the speeches attributed to saints exhibit little or no stylistic variation. They are mainly scriptural phrases strung together to fit the occasion. Apparently the doctrine of rhetorical decorum, though perfectly suited to the saint's ability to address all classes in their own idiom, was felt to obscure or compromise the all-important pattern.

II

The genre of saints' lives may be described, then, as the literary analogue of Paul's spiritual genetics. Hagiography preserves the line of Christ in a succession of living patterns, so that we, in Paul's words, "beholding the glory of the Lord with open face [might be] transformed into the same image" (2 Cor. 3.18).

But how does this transformation work? We can adopt the life pattern of a biblical hero, even his way of speaking, but it does not follow that we will be *transformed*. The Bible itself treats the question in several ways, but two in particular stand out.

The first involves the figure of a mirror, as in the following seminal passage (James 1.23–24):

> For if a man be a hearer of the word and not a doer, he shall be compared to a man beholding his own countenance in a glass. For he beheld himself, and went his way, and presently forgot what manner of man he was.

Medieval commentaries make the comparison between the Bible and the looking-glass explicit: God's word is a *speculum*, reflecting not only the viewer's present self but also his potential self.[19] Assimilation of the real to the ideal requires almost constant attention, however, because most people forget "what manner of man" they are as soon as they turn away.

John Chrysostom was the first, according to Herbert Grabes,

---

[19] See, for example, Hugh of St. Cher, *Opera Omnia in Universum Vetus et Novum Testamentum* (Lyons, 1668), 7:313 (col. 4).

to extend the metaphor to the lives of saints.[20] There is a mirror, Chrysostom writes,

> [that] not only shews our own deformity, but transforms it too, if we be willing, into surpassing beauty. This mirror is the memory of good men, and the history of their blessed lives; the reading of the Scriptures; the laws given by God. If thou be willing once only to look upon the portraitures of those holy men, thou wilt both see the foulness of thine own mind, and having seen this, wilt need nothing else to be set free from that deformity. Because the mirror is useful for this purpose also, and makes the change easy.[21]

Here in a nutshell is the rationale behind the countless "mirrors" that proliferated during the Middle Ages and Renaissance, mirrors of morality for every class of people: *Speculum laicorum, Speculum monachorum, Speculum sacerdotum, Speculum regum,* and so forth.[22] All purport to show the reader an unflattering view of himself or an ideal model of the self or both. The object is transformation. In the *Speculum fidei*, William of St. Thierry says that the reader must "show himself to himself" in order that he might "through the exertion of piety gradually be conformed to the spiritual and divine reality occupying his thoughts."[23] In her brief memoir, which Peter Dronke puts in the genre of "mirrors for princes," Dhuoda (b. 803) presents a choice of patterns (including the biblical Joseph) for her sixteen-year-old son:

> Your Dhuoda is always there to encourage you, my son, and when I am gone, which will come to pass, you'll have

---

[20] *The Mutable Glass,* trans. Gordon Collier (Cambridge, 1982). For shorter discussions of the mirror image in medieval literature, see the articles by Sister Ritamary Bradley, "Backgrounds of the Title *Speculum* in Medieval Literature," *Speculum* 29 (1954): 100–15; and "The Speculum Image in Medieval Mystical Writers," in *The Medieval Mystical Tradition in England,* ed. Marion Glasscoe (Cambridge, 1984), 9–27.

[21] Grabes, 95.

[22] Grabes provides in his Appendix (235–329) a useful "synoptic listing of mirror-titles."

[23] *The Mirror of Faith,* trans. Thomas Davis (Kalamazoo, MI, 1979), 34.

the little book of moral teaching here as a memorial: you
will be able to look at me still, as into a mirror, reading me
with your mind and your body and praying to God.[24]

The prologue to the pseudo-Bonaventuran *Speculum vitae Christi*
explains that the book is called a mirror because "through
repeated and intensive contemplation of the exemplar [Christ],
one may approach perfection."[25]

The assumption behind the figure of the mirror is, clearly,
that one becomes more and more *like* the thing one contemplates. The second theory of self-transformation offered by the
Bible relies on a similar logic. Wherever the New Testament
contains the word *imitari*, as in Paul's exhortation "Be ye imitators of me," the commentaries often refer us to Genesis 30.34–
43, the story of Jacob's genetic experiments with the sheep and
goats of his father-in-law, Laban. The situation is this: Jacob has
offered to tend Laban's flock in return for the seemingly modest
wages of the spotted animals.

And Laban said: I like well what thou demandest.

And he separated the same day the she goats, and the
sheep, and the he goats, and the rams of divers colours,
and spotted. . . .

And Jacob took green rods of poplar, and of almond, and
of plane trees, and pilled them in part: so when the bark
was taken off, in the parts that were pilled, there appeared
whiteness: but the parts that were whole remained green:
and by this means the colour was divers.

And he put them in the troughs, where the water was
poured out: that when the flocks should come to drink,
they might have the rods before their eyes, and in the sight
of them might conceive.

And it came to pass that in the very heat of coition, the
sheep beheld the rods, and brought forth spotted, and of
divers colours, and speckled. . . .

And the man was enriched exceedingly, and he had

---

[24] *Women Writers of the Middle Ages* (Cambridge, 1984), 44.
[25] Grabes, 51.

many flocks, maidservants and menservants, camels and asses.

The genetic principle illustrated by Jacob's practice has a venerable history, attested, for example, by classical authorities, the church fathers, and numerous biblical commentators.

Pliny in his *Natural History* (7.12.52) states the theory as follows:

> Cases of likeness are indeed an extremely wide subject, and one which includes the belief that a great many accidental circumstances are influential—recollections of sights and sounds and actual sense-impressions received at the time of conception.[26]

Stories illustrating the belief abound. Hippocrates is said to have saved a woman accused of adultery—her baby looked nothing like the presumed father—by asking "if by chance such a picture were in the woman's bedroom, which, being found, the woman was freed from punishment and suspicion." Quintilian, the famous advocate and rhetorician, is reported to have used a similar defense in the case of a woman who gave birth to a black child; in the heat of coition, he argued, his client had happened to look upon the image of an Ethiopian. She was acquitted.[27]

Biblical commentators on Genesis 30 use such tales as the above (both the accounts of Hippocrates and of Quintilian are exegetical commonplaces) to buttress their moral interpretation of Jacob's experiment. We are the sheep. The stripped rods are the lives of the prophets, patriarchs, and saints. By contemplating their good works, we give birth to good works of our own. The rods are partly peeled and straked because the biographies

---

[26] Trans. H. Rackham, Loeb Classical Library (Cambridge, MA, 1942), 541.

[27] The examples of Hippocrates and Quintilian are cited repeatedly by biblical commentators; see, for example, Hugh of St. Cher on 1 Cor. 11.1, *Opera Omnia*, 7:101 (col. 3); and on Gen. 30, Rupert of Deutz, *Opera* (Venice, 1748), 1:128; Denis the Carthusian, *Opera Omnia* (Montreuil, 1896), 1:345–46; Cornelius a Lapide, *Commentaria in Scripturam Sacram* (Paris, 1865), 1:253–54.

of our models should also be straked, that is, the outer bark of incidental words and deeds stripped away, so that we may look only upon the inner life and outer deeds worthy of emulation.[28]

The moral interpretation of Jacob's experiment, like the *speculum* metaphor, underscores the belief that one can transform the self through sustained contemplation of a model. Between the two explanations, however, there is an essential difference. Dressing one's "self" before the mirror of Scripture or the Life of a saint—discarding certain habits, putting on others—implies the constant engagement of the will. The "scientific" or genetic explanation of pattern-transfer suggests an almost subconscious process, which, once activated by the will, works itself out according to the laws of nature. The observation is not gratuitous but goes to the very heart of medieval assumptions about the self; and it is partly an answer to modern objections that the self is more than a willed assemblage of attributes and actions. What, after all, has the adoption of certain behavioral patterns to do with internal change? Are we not affective beings? Do we not feel joy and grief, hope and despair, love and hate?

The medieval practice of self-fashioning did not overlook the claims of the emotions. The real issue was priority. From a certain disposition of acts, it was believed, there would arise a certain disposition of feelings. This belief manifested itself institutionally in monastic discipline, the orders of knighthood, and so forth, and most personally in the regimen of affective mysticism. For every form of structured life, there was a set of corresponding emotions. Indeed, only within the structured life were certain emotions thought possible. The spiritual "dryness," the "dark night of the soul," the ecstasy of divine union felt by the mystic, for example, were hardly ordinary experiences; they belonged to, and arose out of, a particular form of living. Even love was regarded not as an independent stirring of the will but rather as a feeling or virtue defined through or in response to specific acts, apart from which it could hardly be imagined.

---

[28] See Hugh of St. Cher's exposition, 1:42 (col. 3).

Thus love of God was seen as not only the cause but also the effect of a certain way of life. "Love," Bonaventure says, "is born of obedience to the Law."[29]

This is, in fact, the major lesson of *Piers Plowman*, which may be called an allegory of the will in search of a self.[30] Repeatedly we are told that law is the matrix of love. Piers directs pilgrims to the castle of Truth by way of the Ten Commandments,

> And if grace graunte þee to go in in þis wise
> Thow shalt see in þiselue truþ sitte in þyn herte
> In a cheyne of charite as þow a child were.   (B.5.605–7)

When Will expresses the desire also to meet charity, he is given, in effect, the same advice: "Wiþouten help of Piers Plowman [the incarnation of perfect obedience] his persone sestow neuere" (B.15.196). Love and law exist in synergistic relation. Love may foster the desire to obey, but it is only within a clearly defined system of law that love can realize and express itself fully: "Ac oure lord aloueth no loue but lawe be þe cause" (C.17.136). Thus, the goal of Will—of any will seeking salvation—is assimilation to the Piers-model or conformity to the life-structure called Dowel, which gives birth to Dobet and both in turn to Dobest, successive patterns that embrace not only an ever widening capacity for good works but also an ever deepening potential for psychological and spiritual growth.

The notion that one can transform the self by imitating the lives of saints does not deny the affective component; instead it assumes that a will fixed on the example of Daniel or Paul or Cecilia is more likely to produce the desired feelings and virtues than a will that is not.

---

[29] *Collations*, 3.

[30] For a general discussion, see my chapter "The Design of the Poem" in John A. Alford, ed., *A Companion to Piers Plowman* (Berkeley, 1988), 29–65.

III

To *arrange* a life after the fact is common hagiographical practice. Indeed, Bonaventure openly acknowledges his method:

> Nor have I always woven together the history according
> unto chronology, that I might avoid confusion, but I rather
> endeavoured to preserve a more coherent order, setting
> down sometimes facts of divers kinds that belong unto the
> same period, sometimes facts of the same kind that belong
> unto divers periods, as they seemed best to fit in together
> (*The Life of St. Francis*, 305).

It did not occur to Bonaventure that he was distorting the truth;
on the contrary, his purpose was to enhance the truth, to make
it shine forth with greater clarity and brilliance. Historiogra-
phers, Beryl Smalley reminds us, had much the same attitude:
"The Frisians, comparing themselves to the chosen people,
inverted the order of events in their history, so as to get a closer
correspondence with the Old Testament."[31] According to this
point of view, there is no truth in mere chronology. The lives of
individuals and of nations find their meaning not in some inner
dynamic of their own but rather in their alignment with an
external pattern, such as the template of Scripture.

The belief is not confined to biographers writing after the fact.
The early *imitatores Christi*, Erich Auerbach notes, strove to
follow not only the commandments of Jesus but also his very
destiny.[32] Reviving the practice, St. Francis placed himself in a
typological relation to Scripture. Its patterns were more real for
him than the accidents of contemporary life. Even through the
conventionality of most accounts, we catch a glimpse of this fact
now and then. For example, when the dying Francis broke
bread with his followers for the last time, he asked, wishing to

---

[31] *The Study of the Bible in the Middle Ages* (1952; repr. Notre Dame,
1964), xi.
[32] Erich Auerbach, *Scenes from the Drama of European Literature*, trans.
Ralph Manheim and C. Garvin (New York, 1959), 95.

stress the parallelism with the Last Supper: "Is it Thursday?"[33] Christina of Markyate also lived in the Bible. She was particularly fond of the Thirty-seventh Psalm, about which her biographer observes: "A very suitable passage and one that described the situation of the reader; this she repeated often, lamenting at one moment her own weakness and blindness, at another the violence and guile of her parents, friends, and relatives, who were seeking her life" (93). There can be little doubt that many medieval people found significance in their lives chiefly to the extent that they fulfilled certain biblical paradigms.

Richard Rolle, a fourteenth-century hermit who tried to live as a saint but never attained sainthood, presents an especially interesting case history. His biography, written in anticipation of his being canonized, is complemented by the autobiography of his own extensive writings.[34] The evidence of one is qualified or reinforced by that of the other. Taken together, the two kinds of evidence suggest that many of the scriptural parallels in the hermit's life were created deliberately and not discovered in retrospect. That is, he partly *staged* the chronology of his life, which appears to have been a series of calculated gestures.[35]

---

[33] The *"Mirror of Perfection"*, 263.

[34] The *Officium*, our main biographical source, has been translated by Frances M. Comper, *The Life of Richard Rolle* (1928; repr. New York, 1969), 301–14; and by Hope Emily Allen, *Writings Ascribed to Richard Rolle, Hermit of Hampole* (New York, 1927), 55–61. For a general survey of the scholarship on Rolle, see my chapter "Richard Rolle and Related Works" in A. S. G. Edwards, ed., *Middle English Prose: A Critical Guide to Major Authors and Genres* (New Brunswick, NJ, 1984), 35–60. Among mystical writers of the Middle Ages, Rolle is by no means unique in his use of the Bible for self definition. See, for example, G. Lüers, *Die Sprache der deutschen Mystik des Mittelalters im Werke der Mechthild von Magdeburg* (Munich, 1926; repr. Darmstadt, 1966); Ernst Benz, *Die Vision: Erfahrungsformen und Bilderwelt* (Stuttgart, 1969); Jean Leclercq, *The Love of Learning and the Desire for God*, trans. Catharine Misrahi (New York, 1961), and numerous articles by the same author, including "Lecture et oraison," *La Vie Spirituelle* 70 (1944): 392–402, and "Les méditations d'un moine du XIIe siècle," *Revue Mabillon* 34 (1944): 1–19.

[35] Several of the following paragraphs on Rolle are taken from my article "The Biblical Identity of Richard Rolle," *Fourteenth-Century English Mystics Newsletter* 2 (1976): 21–25 (quoted by kind permission of the editors).

Consider the dramatic opening of his career, as reported in the *Officium de Sancto Ricardo Heremita*:

[A]fter he had returned from Oxford to his father's house, he said one day to his sister ..., "My beloved sister, thou hast two tunics which I greatly covet, one white and the other grey. Therefore I ask thee if thou wilt kindly give them to me, and bring them me to-morrow to the wood near by, together with my father's rain-hood." She agreed willingly, and the next day, according to her promise, carried them to the said wood, being quite ignorant of what was in her brother's mind. And when he had received them he straightway cut off the sleeves from the grey tunic and the buttons from the white, and as best he could he fitted the sleeves to the white tunic, so that they might in some manner be suited to his purpose. Then he took off his own clothes with which he was clad and put on his sister's white tunic next his skin, but the grey, with the sleeves cut out, he put on over it, and put his arms through the holes which had been cut; and he covered his head with the rain-hood aforesaid, so that thus in some measure, as far as was then in his power, he might present a certain likeness to a hermit. But when his sister saw this she was astounded and cried: "My brother is mad! My brother is mad!" Whereupon he drove her from him with threats, and fled himself at once without delay, lest he should be seized by his friends and acquaintances.[36]

The most striking thing about this story is its extraordinary detail, suggesting the extent to which Richard had thought out his plan ahead of time. He asked for a white tunic, a grey tunic, and his father's rainhood; and he knew exactly what he wanted to do with them. There is nothing spontaneous in the account— except perhaps for his sister's reaction ("My brother is mad!"), and even this may have been precisely what Rolle had antici- pated. After all, one of his favorite themes, borrowed from St. Paul, is that the wisdom of Christ appears as foolishness in the

---

[36] *The Life of Richard Rolle*, 301–2.

eyes of the world.[37] This is, in fact, a *topos* of the genre. To be ridiculed or misunderstood—especially by one's own family—is the hallmark of a saint in the first stage of his career.

Following the *lectio* quoted above, there is a response, "The saint has fled to solitude," which suggests a parallelism with the life of Christ, who prepared for his ministry in the same way. This parallelism is strengthened in the next *lectio*.

> After having thus put on the habit of a hermit and left his parents, he went to a certain church.... And when the gospel had been read in the mass, having first besought the blessing of the priest, he went into the preacher's pulpit and gave the people a sermon of wonderful edification, insomuch that the multitude which heard it was so moved by his preaching that they could not refrain from tears; and they all said that they had never before heard a sermon of such virtue and power.[38]

That the young Richard would have received the priest's permission on the spot is highly improbable. Like the meeting with his sister, he must have prearranged this too. The significant point is that Rolle carefully chose to begin his ministry in the same way as Christ, who also, after a period of solitude in the wilderness "went into the synagogue according to his custom on the sabbath day; and he rose up to read" (Luke 4.16).

Then follows another parallel. After mass the young hermit was invited to dinner by one of his listeners, Sir John de Dalton (who would later become his first patron):

> [B]ut when he entered his manor he betook himself to a certain mean and old room; for he would not enter the hall, but sought rather to fulfil the teaching of the gospel, which says, "When thou art invited to a wedding, sit down in the

---

[37] See, for example, *The Contra Amatores Mundi of Richard Rolle of Hampole*, ed. and trans. Paul Theiner, University of California Publications, English Studies 33 (Berkeley, 1968), 149, 169, 183, and passim.

[38] *The Life of Richard Rolle*, 302.

lowest room; that when he that bade thee cometh, he may say unto thee, Friend, go up higher," and this too was fulfilled in him. For when the squire had sought for him diligently, and at last found him in the aforesaid room, he set him above his own sons at the table.[39]

The parallels continue. But instead of enlarging the inventory, let me simply comment on one final example. Rolle talks a great deal about his enemies. In fact, if we accept all of his complaints literally—as Hope Emily Allen did[40]—then he must have been one of the most harassed and persecuted human beings who ever lived. I doubt that he was. His "enemies" were a biblical necessity. Did not Christ say, for example, "Woe to you when men shall bless you"? Rolle echoes the idea when he says, "[T]he persecutions of our enemies [are] useful and necessary for us ... lest, having no persecutor, we deserve no crown."[41] Now I do not mean to imply that in reality Rolle had no enemies—that he simply manufactured them—or worse yet that he deliberately antagonized people so that they might serve as unwitting testimony to his own sainthood! His enemies were undoubtedly real, but his habit of assimilating everything as biblical history gave them epic proportions, symbolic as well as literal. They are not merely the enemies of Rolle personally; they are the *detractores Deo odibiles* mentioned by St. Paul in Romans 1.30. In another place, Rolle says:

Truly the more these wretches contend against one of God's saints with worthless words, the more they bury themselves in ever greater evils. Blinded by their wickedness they wilfully abandon one whom they could have had to intercede for them before God. And so, amid disgrace, amid mockery and slander, amid censure and hatred, boldly he sings with the Psalmist: "Let my judgment come forth from thy countenance O good Jesus; let thy eyes

---

[39] *The Life of Richard Rolle*, 303.
[40] *Writings Ascribed to Richard Rolle*, 470–88.
[41] *Contra Amatores Mundi*, 158.

behold the things that are equitable. Thou hast proved my heart, and visited it by night, thou hast tried me by fire: and iniquity hath not been found in me" [Ps. xvi. 2–3].[42]

In a passage like this, in which Rolle assumes the identity of the Psalmist, first implicitly and then by direct quotation, it is impossible to measure the depth or sincerity of his emotions. He is playing out a script written centuries earlier by several biblical heroes. Insofar as he reveals himself at all, he appears as a composite of these men. Was he contentious? Then so was Job. Was he vindictive in tone? Then so was David. Was he presumptuous in referring to himself as a saint? Then so was Paul. Most of his apparently autobiographical remarks are quotations or paraphrases from the Bible. We must be extremely cautious, therefore, in making inferences about the man on the basis of his writings. Even if we were able to distinguish the echo from the voice, the gesture from the felt emotion, could Rolle have done so himself?

In recent years, we have seen a great deal written on earlier concepts of the self (the names of Colin Morris, John Benton, Karl Weintraub, Robert Hanning, Caroline Bynum, and Stephen Greenblatt come immediately to mind). It is generally agreed that medieval and modern views of the self differ radically. It has even been doubted that our ancestors had any notion of a "core personality." They tended to see themselves less as individuals than as individual manifestations of well-known and codified forms of behavior—in short, as adapted stereotypes. On the one hand, this point of view limited the variety of self-expression; but on the other, it freed many men and women to adopt, within certain bounds, *personae* of their own choosing. I have tried to show that the Bible played an important role in the process. One could hope to be another Joseph, another Ruth. Through assimilation to a biblical exemplar, one could learn properly to think, to feel, actually to achieve a self. St. Paul expresses the fundamental optimism of Christian psychology in his famous exhortation to the Ephesians (4.22–24): "To put off,

---

[42] *Contra Amatores Mundi*, 150.

according to former conversation, the old man, who is corrupt-
ed according to the desire of error ... and [to] put on the new
man, who according to God is created in justice and holiness of
truth." In the Middle Ages, at least, people were prepared to
take the Apostle's words literally.

The Bible as Thesaurus
for Secular Literature

Joan M. Ferrante

The Bible is a treasure house for medieval writers, a virtually inexhaustible source of exemplary figures, cautionary tales, and quotable lines for any occasion; the same can be said of much classical Latin literature, which is used at least to the same extent by most secular writers. One might expect a difference in approach to the two sources, but in practice both are treated with a reverence for authority and at the same time a disregard for accuracy of text or context. Despite the well-known medieval respect for the authority of the word, there is actually a great deal of freedom in the invoking of it. Perhaps because God's Word took on human form, both in language in the books of the Bible, and in history in the person of Christ, medieval man felt free to invest it with his own meanings and his own purposes.

Others have written on serious (or religious) use and parody of the Bible in secular literature; some have read religious allegory into secular texts, on the assumption perhaps that if a work contains religious allusions it must have a religious message. What I will focus on here is the a-religious, irreligious, or anti-religious (at least anti-clerical) use of the Bible in secular literature—by secular literature I mean non-religious literature whether written by laymen or clerics. This is not to deny a traditional moral or religious use of biblical figures and verses in secular literature, but to concentrate on other possibilities, on their function in making political statements, in enhancing love stories, in supporting pleas for love or money, in criticizing clerical defects, or simply in titillating the audience.

The biblical figures who are named most frequently in secular literature are Adam as an example of pride and as the *terminus a quo* for time ("not since Adam has there been . . ."), Eve as responsible for the Fall and the loss of Paradise, Cain and Abel as the envious treacherous fratricide and the innocent victim, Solomon as the source of wisdom (much of it anti-feminist and frequently cited), Judas as the arch-betrayor and a figure of greed and despair, and David, as the defeater of the giant, the strong ruler, the wise man, the deceived lover, or the grieving father and friend. But the traditional identifications do not preclude other possibilities. Solomon is not only the wise man, he can also be the deceived lover: "O tu, de nome Amor . . . Chè Sanson decedesti e Salamone" (Guittone d'Arezzo, 1.7.65: "You, Love by name . . . you deceived Samson and Solomon").[1] Eve may be blamed by most writers for the Fall, but Gottfried von Strassburg suggests that God's prohibition made her disobedience inevitable (*Tristan*, 17934 ff.), and though Dante the pilgrim blames her throughout Purgatory (*Purg.* 8.99, 12.71, 29.24), the heavenly procession, which includes the books of the Bible, names Adam, as if to remind Dante that each man is responsible for his own fall (*Purg.* 32.37).

Dante describes a number of biblical figures in their traditional roles; Judas as the betrayor, Nembrot as the proud rebel, Rachel and Leah as the contemplative and the active life, the Virgin Mary as an example of every virtue and the protector of mankind.[2] But he neither presents as many biblical figures as

---

[1] *Poeti del Duecento*, ed. Gianfranco Contini (Milan: Ricciardi, 1960), 2 vols. All Italian lyrics cited in the text are from this edition. References will henceforth be given in the text by poet, volume, poem, and line number. Translations are mine unless otherwise noted.

[2] Nathan, Joshua, Judas Maccabeus, Hezekiah, are seen in different spheres of Paradise, and Sarah, Rebecca, Rachel, Ruth, Judith, Eve, and Moses are seen in the rose, but they do not speak to Dante. The edition of the *Divine Comedy* which will be referred to in this paper is the

one might expect nor does he always present them in the expected way. Among the many souls featured (rather than just mentioned) in Paradise, the biblical are only a handful: Rahab, the prostitute who helped Joshua conquer the Holy Land, is a figure for the church which, as Dante shows throughout the poem, is currently prostituting itself (e.g., *Inf.* 19.106–8 and *Purg.* 32.148–60). Solomon, seen among the great teachers of the church, is the height of human wisdom because he asked only for sufficient wisdom to be king (*Par.* 13.95–96). Adam is the originator of human speech (*Par.* 26); Peter, the first pope, denounces the modern papacy (*Par.* 27); David is not only the ruler who embodies divine justice (*Par.* 20) but also the fool before God (*Purg.* 10), a figure of great humility, and most important, he is the poet, the "cantor de lo spirito santo" (*Par.* 20.38), the "umile salmista" (*Purg.* 10.64).

Dante, himself a chosen poet of God, alludes to a number of biblical episodes to give divine sanction to his message. The Exodus journey is his model for Purgatory, the passage from the slavery of Egypt (sin) to the salvation of the promised land which Dante adds to the paradigm he used in Hell, the national movement of the Trojans from the fallen city towards the founding of Rome. But Exodus does not replace the *Aeneid*, which is still a model in Paradise. For Dante, unlike Augustine, both the Jews and the Romans are God's chosen people (see *Monarchia*, book 2, *Convivio*, book 4), one in the religious, the other in the political sphere, so he couples examples of the virtues and vices from the Bible with examples from classical antiquity throughout Purgatory. But he also invokes the apocryphal Harrowing of Hell, when Christ rescued a group of Old Testament figures, in his Limbo of virtuous pagans, in order to register a difference between those who believed in the Messiah and those who did not. Dante seems to expect his audience to be able to supply biblical texts from the brief allusions he makes, as in *Purg.* 2.46–48, when the souls sing " 'In exitu Israel de Aegypto' ... con quanto di quel salmo é poscia scripto"

Petrocchi text as presented by Charles S. Singleton, (Princeton: Princeton University Press, 1970–75).

("with the rest of the psalm as it is written"); or *Purg.* 30.83–84, when the angels sing " 'In te, Domine speravi,' / ma oltre 'pedes meos' non passaro" ("but did not go beyond 'pedes meos' "). It is not, therefore, unlikely that he might expect his audience to supply parts of an episode without his alluding to it directly, as in *Inf.* 2, when he says he is neither Aeneas nor Paul, describing Aeneas as the one chosen by heaven to be the father of Rome and of its empire which was established as the seat of the papacy, and calling Paul the "chosen vessel," the "Vas d'elezione" (28), a phrase which comes from Acts 9.15. In the same chapter of Acts, another Aeneas, who has lain in bed with palsy for eight years, is cured by Peter in the name of Christ (9.34). Dante may well have read this to mean that the Christian faith would restore the pagan empire, and he expected his reader to take the same lesson, again connecting the biblical message with the destiny of Rome.

Wolfram von Eschenbach, who was also concerned with the conversion of pagans, puts the biblical examples to rather unusual uses in the mouths of pagan characters in his *Willehalm*. Guiborc, the hero's wife, a convert, asks the Christian princes to have mercy on the conquered pagans by identifying with them:

> ein heiden was der êrste man,
> den got machen began.
> Nû geloupt, daz Êljias und Ênoch
> vür heiden sint behalden noch.
> Nôê ouch ein heiden was,
> der in der arken genas.
> Jôp vür wâr ein heiden hiez,
> den got dar umme niht verstiez.
> . . . .
> wir wâren doch alle heidensch ê.
>
> (6.306.29–307.25)

The first man that God made was a heathen. Believe me, Elias and Enoch, though they were heathens, are still alive. Noah too was a heathen who was saved in the ark. A heathen likewise was Job, whom God did not for that reason reject. . . . We were all heathens once.[3]

---

[3] The German text is from Wolfram von Eschenbach, *Willehalm*, ed.

Her pagan father, however, makes a speech of a very different
sort, in response to his son's Christian propaganda:

> hân ich dich durch den verlorn,
> den sîn selbes künne hienc
> und unprîs an im begienc,
> zuo dem hân ich kleinen trôst,
> daz unser vater würde erlôst,
> Adâm, von hellebanden
> mit menneschlîchen handen.
>
>   (5.219.6–12)

If I have lost you because of Him Whom His own race
hanged and disgraced, I have small confidence about His
delivering our father Adam from the bonds of hell with his
human hands.

For all his scepticism, the father seems to be well versed in the
Bible, since he later says "It deeply troubles me, *as I have read*,
that David also warred with his son" (7.355.12–14: "aller sêrest
mich nû müet, / ich hân gelesen, daz Dâvit / gein sînem kinde
ouch hête strît").

The Bible is much invoked in *Willehalm* and its *chansons de
geste* counterparts in the Guillaume cycle. Christian warriors are
given to prayers in moments of stress, which sound like capsule
versions of the Bible:

> Glorios Deus, qui me fesistes né
> Fesis la terre tot a ta volenté
> . . . .
> Adam formas et puis Evain sa per;
> En paradis les en menas ester;
> Li fruiz des arbres lor fu abandonez,
> Fors d'un pomier, icil lor fu veez;
> Il en mangierent, ce fu grant foleté. . . .
>
>   (695–702)[4]

Albert Leitzmann (Tübingen: Max Niemeyer, 1956). The translation is by
Charles E. Passage (New York: Ungar, 1977).

[4] The French text is from *Le Couronnement de Louis*, ed. Ernest
Langlois (Paris: Champion, 1966).

Glorious God, who created me and the earth to your will
.... You formed Adam, and then Eve, his mate, and let
them live in Paradise; they had the fruits of all trees except
for one apple, that was forbidden; but they ate it, and that
was madness. . . .

And so on for a total of ninety-four lines, going through the
Flood, Christ's birth, the Slaughter of the Innocents, the Tempta-
tion in the Desert, the Passion (in some detail), the Deposition,
and the Harrowing of Hell. At crucial moments in the midst of
battle, instead of seeing their lives pass before them, Christian
heroes see the Bible. Not surprisingly, the biblical episodes most
frequently invoked on the battlefield are those which involve
great suffering and danger and eventual rescue: the children in
the furnace, Daniel, Jonah, Lazarus, Mary Magdalene, and
Christ in death and resurrection. But in one intriguing case,
Rainoart prays at length to God for protection and victory, with
the standard series of biblical stories, and is nearly killed by his
opponent; then he blurts out a quick line and a half to the
Virgin, "Sainte Virge hennoré, / Secorez-moi, roine coroné"
(172, J.6838–9), and his power is redoubled.[5] I do not know
what if any conclusions we are meant to draw from this, or if it
is just a dramatic device, but it is effective.

In fact, the greatest number of biblical references in literature
are single-verse quotations. The most interesting examples are
in parodies or attacks on clerical corruption (which I will
discuss later), but even when they are cited in support of
traditional moral positions, it is often without any concern for
authenticity. Numerous lines are attributed to Scripture or
specifically to Solomon, sometimes with no more justification
than the desire to lend authority to the poet's position. Marca-

---

[5] The text is from *Aliscans*, ed. M. Jonckbloet, *Guillaume d'Orange* (La
Haye: Nyhoff, 1854). Michelne de Combarieu, "Les prières à la vierge
dans l'épopée," in *La Prière au Moyen-Age*, Senefiance 10 (Paris: Champion, 1981), 91–120, notes that some heroes feel the need to address both
God and the Virgin Mary, and that the general prayer to God may be
followed by a direct one to the Virgin (98) and concludes that prayers
to her only work because she is a mediator (113); but this does not alter
the effect in this scene, particularly since Rainoart is a pagan.

bru, who describes himself as a chastiser of vice and a sower of words, in apparent imitation of Christ (Matt. 13.4), does not hesitate to use Scripture loosely: "Non cuich que'l segles dur gaire / segon qu'escriptura di" (17.3–4: "I don't think the world will last much longer, as Scripture says").[6] "Aprop lo bon lanz vos gardaz / ço diz Salomons e Daviz" (6.31–32: "after a good throw [of the dice], watch out, that's what Solomon and David say"). Peire Cardenal claims that those who confess and repent will be blessed in paradise and the false burned in the fires of hell, "if I don't say true, then Scripture lies" (78.27: "S'ieu non dic ver, doncx l'escriptura men"),[7] but his claim is only vaguely based on scriptural texts (2 Thes. 1.4–10; James 3.6).

Solomon is frequently invoked for anti-feminist attacks, sometimes accurately, sometimes not: on the false whore, Marcabru quotes Prov. 5.3–4 fairly closely, "Solomon says, and bears witness to it, that at first she is sweet as mead, but when you depart she is more stinging, bitter, and cruel than a serpent" (44.9–12: "Salemos ditz et es guirens / c'al prim es dousa cum pimens / mas al partir es plus cozens / amar' e cruzels cum serpens.") When the *Roman de la Rose* cites Solomon: "Salemon dist c'onc ne fu ... riens de fame plus ireuse, / n'onc riens, ce dit, n'ot tant malice"[8] (16300–303: "Solomon says that nothing is angrier than a woman, nothing has such malice"), it begins fairly close to Ecclus. 25.22–26, but as the passage continues "... Si redit ailleurs l'escriture / que de tout le femenin vice / li fondemanz est avarice" (16313–16: "elsewhere Scripture says that the root of all female vice is avarice"), it turns a general statement about avarice (1 Tim. 6.10) into a direct attack on women. Similarly the source of "Si dit Salemon toutevois, /

---

[6] The text is from *Poèsies Complètes du Troubadour Marcabru*, ed. J. M. L. Dejeanne (Toulouse: Privat, 1909). Laura Kendrick, in her dissertation, "Criticism of the Ruler, 1100–1400" (Columbia University, 1978), 70 ff., discusses Marcabru assuming the persona of the priest and reinforcing his words with biblical citations.

[7] The text is from *Poèsies Complètes du Troubador Peire Cardenal*, ed. René Lavaud (Toulouse: Privat, 1957).

[8] The text is from the edition by Félix Lecoy (Paris: Champion, 1965–70).

puis que par la verité vois, / que beneurez hom seroit / qui
bone fame troveroit" (RR. 18119–22: "Solomon, however, says,
since I go by the truth, that blessed would the man be who
found a good woman"), does not use the conditional with its
implication of impossibility. Ecclesiasticus 26.1 says "Mulieris
bonae beatus vir; . . . Mulier fortis oblectat vir suum et annos
vitae illius in pace implebit" ("blessed is the husband of a good
woman . . . a strong woman delights her man and will fill the
years of his life in peace"), which implies that such women do
exist.

Dante accurately cites a line attributed to Solomon, but sets it
in a startling context. He has the souls he sees in the heaven of
Jupiter first spell out the words "Diligite justiciam qui judicatis
terram" (18.91–93: "Love justice you who judge the earth")
from the Book of Wisdom, 1.1, and then, out of the final *m* in
terram, form the imperial Roman eagle, implying that divine
justice is manifest on earth through the Roman Empire. Dante
uses biblical references not only to set the mood of Hell and
Purgatory (in cantos 1 and 2) and the final vision in Paradise
(*Par.* 30–32), and to reinforce his theological and political argu-
ments, but also to enhance his own stature and that of other
poets. When Farinata addresses Dante in the words of the
woman who questioned Peter (*Inf.* 10.24, based on Matt. 26.73),
the allusion suggests that Dante, like Peter, is temporarily in
error but destined to be a prime teacher of the Word; when
Sordello writes with his finger on the ground (*Purg.* 7.52), he
recalls Christ in John 8.6, 8. When Statius (the Roman and, as
far as we know, pagan poet) appears to Dante and Virgil in
Purgatory, his appearance is heralded by the sound of "Gloria
in excelsis . . . Deo," first heard when the angels announced
Christ's birth (Luke 2.8–14), as Dante reminds us (*Purg.* 20.136);
the meeting of the poets is compared with Christ's encounter
with his disciples on the road to Emmaus (Luke 24.13–16), to
which Dante makes specific reference: "come ne scrive Luca /
che Cristo apparve a' due ch'erano in via" (*Purg.* 21.7–8: "as
Luke writes that Christ appeared to the two on the road"). Once
again this suggests that Dante, not to say Virgil, is an apostle of
God's word,[9] perhaps even that the poet is a Christ figure who

---

[9] Christopher Kleinhenz, "Iconographic Parody in *Inferno* 21," *Res*

manifests God's word to men. Virgil was, of course, thought to have prophesied Christ's birth in his fourth eclogue.

To some extent any poet who uses biblical material is adapting it to his own purposes, but presumably not all believe, as Dante clearly does, that he is also serving God's purpose, that his poem is a divinely appointed mission. Prudentius seems to be serving God's purpose in his *Psychomachia*, where he interprets parts of the Abraham story as a "figura" for our life. When, however, a romance poet like Hartmann von Aue uses Job as the model for his *Arme Heinrich*, the intent is not so clear. His hero does not patiently accept God's will; indeed, he tries all medical resources before he gives up and resigns himself to God's will and even then he allows himself to be persuaded to accept the sacrifice of a child. Only when he sees the naked body of the girl who must be killed in order to save him does he really accept God's will. As he looks at her very beautiful body, Hartmann says somewhat ambiguously, Heinrich gets a "new idea" (1233–35: "ir lîp der was vil minneclich. / nû sach er si an unde sich / und gewan einen niuwen muot").[10] He stops the operation (much to the child's disgust—she wants to be a martyr), and God restores him to health, having tested him like Job (1360–64). Then Heinrich marries the girl, which puts a rather different light on the nature of his conversion. Actually, both characters in this work are saints manqués, their story a parody of two different kinds of saints' lives. One, the Job figure who tries anything rather than accept God's will and is finally converted more by lust than by compassion, the other a would-be martyr who insists on self-sacrifice over the objections of her loving parents and pouts like a spoiled child when she is finally deprived of it. I am not sure what Hartmann was saying in this work; perhaps that the devout as well as the worldly have to accept God's plans for them rather than their own. The

---

Publica Litterarum 5 (1982): 125–37, suggests that Virgil carrying Dante in his arms is based on Christ as the Good Shepherd carrying lost souls, a popular theme in early Christian art, and that he is a counter to the devil carrying sinners into the pitch, who reenacts the Harrowing of Hell, negatively, each time he comes back with a soul.

[10] The text is from *Der arme Heinrich*, ed. Hermann Paul (Tübingen: Niemeyer, 1958).

hero has to temper his pride, the heroine her ambition.

In his *Gregorius*, the story of a great sinner who becomes a saintly pope, Hartmann uses biblical models in yet another way. The devil works through the hero's mother as he did Eve, first so that she attracts the incestuous attentions of her brother, and then so that she is attracted to her own son (ll. 303 ff. and particularly ll. 1960–62). When she discovers that she has married her son, her distress is such that Judas did not suffer more when he hanged himself, nor David when he learned that Saul and Jonathan and his son Absalom were dead (2623 ff.). But despite such dire comparisons Hartmann saves the mother, and her son becomes pope after a seventeen-year penance of indescribable suffering described in graphic detail. There are a number of biblical allusions in Gregorius's penance which for Hartmann's audience would have been associated with the papacy: he spends the entire time chained to a rock ("Thou art Peter and upon this rock I will build my church" [Matt. 16.18]); he is sustained by Christ through the Holy Spirit (3119); the key to the chains has been tossed into the sea by a bad fisherman, but is miraculously found by the same fisherman inside a fish ("And I will give unto thee the keys of the kingdom of heaven" [Matt. 16.19]); "Follow me and I will make you fishers of men" [Matt. 4.19])—Peter, the first pope, was a fisherman and a fisher of men and the fish is an ancient symbol of Christ. These allusions, combined with the fact that the hero, Gregorius, bears the name of a distinguished reform pope, Gregory VII (Hildebrand), suggest that Hartmann is making a statement about the papacy, that the pope may be the worst kind of sinner imaginable, but if, and only if, he repents completely, withdraws from the world (read worldly wealth and power—Gregorius had been a successful knight), and imposes on himself a life of austerity and self-denial, he can nonetheless be a model pope.

In the *Parzival*, a work which may well owe something to *Gregorius*, as well as to Chrétien's *Perceval*, Wolfram makes some of the same allusions; and he adds the apocalyptic imagery that surrounds both the hero's birth and the Grail: his pregnant mother's dream of the dragon at her womb, and her withdrawal to the wilderness (like the woman in labor, threatened by a dragon, who brings forth a child who is to rule all nations, and then flees to the wilderness [Rev. 12]), not to mention Herzeloyde's identification with the Virgin as she nurses her son. Having noted that "humility was her way" (113.16: "diemuot was ir bereit"),[11] Wolfram has her speak of the supreme queen offering her breasts to Jesus, and of the dire consequences to anyone who angers him. The Grail castle changes its location like the new Jerusalem which descends to earth. The throne of the king behind a door, the procession of twenty-four, the stone Grail on which the hero's name will be written, despite his early failure to ask the question—all these recall various details from the Apocalypse: the throne of God behind the door in heaven, the twenty-four attendants, the sea of glass before the throne, no man worthy to open or read the book (Rev. 4, 5), and the lamb's name written that no man knew but himself (19.12). The king of the Grail, whom Parzival is to succeed, is also a fisherman (*vischaere*). Whatever the origins— "pescheur" is both "sinner" and "fisherman" in Middle French —the fact that he is a fisherman must remind us of Peter, particularly since he presides over a society of templars (*templeise*), who are sustained by the Grail which is renewed each Good Friday by a visit of the heavenly dove (9.468–70). The king, Amfortas, bestows a sword on the young hero, perhaps recalling the two swords in Luke 22.38, by which the papacy claimed temporal and spiritual power; and Repanse de Schoye gives him a cloak, which can be a symbol of papal responsibility.[12] Since the only churchmen who appear in the poem are the templars of the Grail and the hermit Trevrizent, and since their mission seems to be to keep order in society and to convert the world to Christianity, what Wolfram may have in mind is a re-

---

[11] The German text is Albert Leitzmann's edition (Tübingen: Niemeyer, 1948–55), 3 vols. There is a recent book on biblical language in *Parzival*, David Duckworth's *The Influence of Biblical Terminology and Thought on Wolfram's "Parzival," with special reference to the Epistle of St. James and the Concept of Zwîvel* (Göppingen: Kümmerle, 1980).

[12] A scarlet cloak was thrown over the elected pope by the archdeacon of the Roman church when he accepted the office; see Walter Ullman, *A Short History of the Papacy in the Middle Ages* (London: Methuen, 1972), 230. Dante uses the image frequently, the "papale ammanto": *Inf.* 2.27, cf. 19.69; *Purg.* 16.129 and 19.104–5.

formed church, headed, as in *Gregorius*, by a repentant sinner, and supported not by a clerical hierarchy but by devoted knights who serve God by serving the world. Popes like Hadrian IV and Innocent III had by this time made claims of secular power for the papacy, to the distress of many secular princes, perhaps including the patrons of Hartmann and Wolfram.

Dante, who wanted a church free of secular wealth and power, offers a negative allegory of the papacy in *Inf.* 13: among the suicides, he meets Pier della Vigna, "Peter of the Vineyard," a perversion of Saint Peter, who died for the vineyard that contemporary popes are laying waste (*Par.* 18.131–32; cf. Matt. 21.28: "Fili, vade hodie, operare in vinea mea"). Pier was the chancellor of Frederick II (Federico, "rich in faith," whom Dante places among the heretics); his court styled itself the "ecclesia imperialis," and Pier della Vigna was its Saint Peter, the rock upon which it was founded.[13] What Dante suggests is a pope abusing the gifts of his office (the keys, *Inf.* 13.58–60) to serve a false faith, and the church using its power to interfere with the functioning of the empire, thereby committing spiritual suicide. In Purgatory, Dante represents the church through angels, who hold the papal symbols, the keys and the sword, and administer the sacrament of penance, but are pure spirit. Throughout the *Comedy*, Dante draws on imagery from the church-state debate, most of which is biblical in origin, to support the cause of the Roman Empire and to deny the church temporal power, even more strongly than he had in the *Monarchia*.[14]

---

[13] For such usage at the imperial court, see William A. Stephany, "Pier della Vigna's Self-Fulfilling Prophecies: The 'Eulogy' of Frederick II and *Inferno* 13," *Traditio* 38 (1982): 193–212. For a discussion of this imagery in relation to Dante's views of the church and of church-state relations, see my *The Political Vision of the Divine Comedy* (Princeton: Princeton University Press, 1984), chapter 2.

[14] Since I have gone into this in some detail in *The Political Vision*, I only mention it here. I would like, however, to note that the Archipoeta had used biblical echoes a century and a half before Dante to support his emperor, Frederick I. He begins one poem, "Salve mundi domine, Cesar noster ave," substituting "mundi domine," "lord of the world," for "dominus caeli," "lord of heaven" (Ps. 32.6), "cesar noster," "our

The use of the Bible in support of secular leaders or states may be justified by their being part of God's design, but its use in the pursuit of worldly love is less easily explained. In the dialogues of Andreas Capellanus, the men use biblical texts to try to persuade the women to accept their love; for example, in the first dialogue: as the heavenly kingdom rejoices over the conversion of one sinner more than ninety-nine just (Luke 15.7), so a woman does better if she takes a man who is none too good and makes him better; and in the eighth dialogue, the man claims he deserves more than the lover who only serves because he asks for love, on the basis of "Ask and it shall be given" (Matt. 7.7; Luke 11.9). The women, on the other hand, use the Bible to reprove the men: "Solomon tells us that all praise in one's own mouth disappears" (Prov. 27.2) and "it is found in Holy Scripture that the higher the position, the greater the fall, if one neglect his duty" (Luke 12.48).[15]

Provençal and Italian lyrics abound in more startling examples: "lauzengiers ... son pejor que Judas, que Dieus trays" (Cercamon, 8.34–35: "scandal-mongers [the lovers' enemies] ... are worse than Judas who betrayed God"); "il vostro nome, ch'é chiamato dea, saria mai sempre chiamato Giudea / a similglianza di Giuda giudeo / che tradì Gesù Cristo per un bascio"

---

emperor," for "pater noster," "our father" (Matt. 6.9), and recalling the "ave gratia plena" to Mary of Luke 1.28. He compares Frederick to God with all three, and in stanza 14 he compares him to Judas Maccabeus. Frederick does God's work, "opus deo gratum," bringing peace to the empire. The text is *Die Gedichte des Archipoeta*, ed. Heinrich Watenphul (Heidelberg: C. Winter, 1958). The poet calls attention to his use of biblical texts by rejecting classical sources: "as a son of the church, I follow a healthy faith, and scorn the vain falseness of the gentiles, so I do not invoke Phoebus or Diana, nor ask the muses for Cicero's tongue" (7.1–4). The Christian material of the poem implies the Christian rightness of the empire. The poem can also be read sarcastically, the poet deriding the emperor's pretensions; see W. T. H. Jackson, "The Politics of a Poet: The Archipoeta As Revealed by His Imagery," in *The Challenge of the Medieval Text* (New York: Columbia University Press, 1985).

[15] Book 1, dialogue 8. For the Latin text see *Andreae Capellani Regii Francorum, De Amore, libri tres*, ed. E. Trojel (1892; repr. Munich: Eidos, 1964); for the English translation, see *The Art of Courtly Love*, trans. John J. Parry (1941; repr. New York: Ungar, 1959).

(Il Mare Amoroso, l. 319–22: "your name, that's called goddess should be called Jewess, like Judas, the Jew who betrayed Jesus Christ for a kiss"); "Sì come i Magi a guida de la stella ... per adorar lo Segnor ... così mi guidò Amore a veder quella" (Lapo Gianni, 2.16.1–4: "as the Magi [were] guided by the star ... to adore the Lord ... so Love guided me to see her"); "qe jai / me posca, de so qe'il deman, / et atrestan tost, Dieus, si'l plai, / co fes vin d'aiga, devenir" (Raimbaut d'Aurenga, 16.45–48: "God could give me joy in what I ask [to possess the lady], and quickly too, if it pleases him, God who made water into wine"); "Dieus retenc lo cel el tro / a sos ops ... / c'a mi donz laisset en patz / c'a seignoriu vas totz latz, / qe'l mons totz li deu servir" (Raimbaut, 30.50–56: "God kept heaven and the firmament for his own use ... and left my lady in peace to rule on all sides, so that all the world would serve her," perhaps a play on "my kingdom is not of this world" [John 18.36]); "pois flori la seca verga / ... tant fina amors ... non cuig q'anc fos" (Arnaut Daniel, 1.25–28: "since the dry rod blossomed [a reference to the Virgin] I think there has not been so fine a love"); and "Dieus ... per que foron assoutas / las falhidas que fetz Longis ... don qu'en un lieg ieu e midons jagam" (Arnaut, 12.25–28: "God, through whom the sins of Longinus were absolved ... grant that my lady and I might lie in one bed").[16]

In the *Vita Nuova*, Dante develops such lyric allusions in a consistent pattern that is even more startling in its implications. He sets Beatrice up as a Christ figure with a series of biblical images: his vision of her death, in chapter 23, which echoes the turbulence of the world at Christ's death (Matt. 27.51–53; Luke

---

[16] The Provençal texts cited in this passage are from *The Poetry of Cercamon and Jaufre Rudel*, ed. George Wolf and Roy Rosenstein (New York: Garland, 1983), *The Life and Works of the Troubadour Raimbaut d'Orange*, ed. W. T. Pattison (Minneapolis: University of Minnesota Press, 1952), and *The Poetry of Arnaut Daniel*, ed. James J. Wilhelm (New York: Garland, 1981). The Italian poems are from Contini, note 1, above. Peter Dronke, in "The Song of Songs and Medieval Love Lyric," in *The Bible and Medieval Culture*, ed. W. Lourdaux and D. Verhelst (Leuven: Leuven University, 1979), 236–62, points out a connection between Guido Cavalcanti's "Chi è questa che vèn" and the Song of Songs (238–39).

23.44–45), followed by the angels rising to heaven with a little white cloud (suggesting the ascension), singing "Osanna in excelsis" (Christ's entry into Jerusalem [Mark 11.10]); his vision of Guido Cavalcanti's lady, Giovanna, also called "Primavera . . . tanto è quanto dire 'prima verrà'" (chap. 24: "Spring . . . as much as to say she will come first"), preceding his own Beatrice just as John the Baptist preceded Christ.[17] Less obvious, but also likely, is a suggestion of the appearance of Christ on the road to Emmaus in Beatrice's appearance between two ladies in chapter 3, after which Dante has a vision of love holding her in his arms, saying "Ego dominus tuus" ("I am your lord") and feeding her his burning heart; in Luke 24, after Christ's appearance to them, the disciples report that their hearts burned within as he spoke. Dante continues the Christ analogy in the *Comedy*, with Beatrice's harrowing of Hell to fetch Virgil; the procession's greeting to Beatrice "Benedictus qui venis" (*Purg.* 30.19: "Blessed are you [masc.] who come" (cf. Matt. 21.9: "Benedictus qui venit in nomine domini"); and her own "Modicum et non videbitis me; / et iterum . . . modicum, et vos videbitis me" (*Purg.* 33.10–12: "A little while and ye shall not see me and again a little while and ye shall see me" [cf. John 16.16]).

Since Dante's love for Beatrice draws him back to God, the analogy if unusual is not unsuitable. Gottfried von Strassburg, on the other hand, suggests that the life and death of a very different pair of lovers is to be a kind of Eucharist, a living bread to all noble hearts (233 ff.). His hero, Tristan, is literally clothed in biblical, particularly Revelation, imagery, both when he is knighted—he fights as God's champion, with shining armor and a horse covered with a white cloth, like the Word of God in Rev. 19—and again when he stands in for Mark at the

---

[17] The text is from the *Vita Nuova*, ed. Michele Barbi, in *Le Opere di Dante* (Florence: Società Dantesca Italiana, 1960). Dante also cites the first lines of the Lamentations of Jeremiah, "Quomodo sedet sola / civitas plena populo. / Facta est quasi vidua domina gentium," after Beatrice's death (chap. 28). He had cited another passage from the Lamentations, 1.12, in chap. 7, after the first shield departed and his setup was spoiled, but there he focused on his own distress, whereas in chap. 28 he is concerned with the public loss.

betrothal to Isot, wearing stones from Rev. 21. As these details recall the Second Coming of Christ and the great battle between good and evil, so Tristan's enemies are all connected with the devil (Morolt, the dragon, Urgan, even Melot), as if he were a savior, and indeed he does save several nations from a terrible enemy (Cornwall from Morolt, Ireland from the dragon, Gilan's land from the giant Urgan).[18]

In certain details of his early life, Tristan also reflects David, the young boy who comes to court, soothes the king with his harp (as David does Saul), and becomes his companion, which adds pathos to their later conflict; he defends the king's people from an overwhelmingly stronger enemy (Goliath is a giant, Morolt has the strength of four men), and is eventually shamed by a love-affair with a married woman. From a moral point of view, the affair might be said to be Tristan's fall from grace, but that is not the way Gottfried treats it. Indeed, just the opposite. Not only does he set the lovers apart from their fellows by their beauty, their talents, and their intellect, but he also describes their time alone in the Minnegrotte as an Eden before the fall, an idyllic existence untroubled by worldly needs or by other people, as if it were only in a social context, only where they are vulnerable to their enemies, that the love becomes sinful. If there is a devil figure in their final fall, it can only be Mark, who tempts them to recklessness by keeping them apart, by his jealous *huote* (surveillance). But they do fall, as if by putting their physical desires before the king's honor and their own, they had profaned their love, transgressed its law: "nu tet er rehte als Adam tete: / daz obez dam ime sin Eve bot, / daz namer und az mit ir den tot" (18162–64: "now he [Tristan] did just as Adam had: he took the fruit that his Eve offered and with it ate his death").[19]

---

[18] On Revelation imagery in the two passages, see my *The Conflict of Love and Honor* (The Hague: Mouton, 1973), 29 and 38–39, and for the enemies as devils, 91–92 and 50.

[19] The text is from *Tristan und Isold*, ed. Friedrich Ranke (Berlin: Weidmann, 1959). Béroul, who treats the physical stage of the affair as a sin, describes the lovers' life during the exile more like life after the Fall, with hunger, fear, and physical suffering.

Even more startling, perhaps, than Gottfried's use of religious imagery for what is an adulterous affair, however exalted intellectually, is Chrétien de Troye's use of Christ's death and resurrection for a hypocritical and adulterous woman (Fenice in *Cligés*), and for a well-meaning but equally adulterous knight (Lancelot), even if Chrétien's tone condemns their action. Fenice, whose name means Phoenix, a bird which symbolizes Christ in his death, resurrection, and eternal life, suffers a martyrdom at the hands of physicians ("li feisoient sosfrir martire" [5941]), appears to die, is buried in a tomb, and brought out to a new life in a kind of Paradise, all to escape her husband and join her lover Cligés, who is said to be the only God who can save her (5635–46: "ele dit que ja n'i avra / mire fors un ... de Deu cuident que ele die, / ... Cligés ... c'est ses Dex qui la puet garir").[20] Lancelot suffers great pains to enter the land of the dead, and rescue those within (like Christ in the Passion and the Harrowing of Hell), and his wounds are treated with the ointment of the three Maries. But it is in that land that Lancelot sleeps with the queen, and Chrétien leaves him imprisoned there, as if he could not bring himself to complete the hero's success after such a fall. Though the function of the Christ imagery in these two works is to show up the idolatry of courtly love it is nonetheless unsettling for that.

Narrative poets, like Gottfried and Chrétien, identify their characters with biblical figures; Dante and lyric poets identify themselves with them. In the *Comedy*, of course, Dante does so out of a sense of responsibility and self-sacrifice, taking on the divine mission to carry God's message. He identifies both with Paul and with Christ: though he begins by saying "Io non Enea, io non Paulo sono" (*Inf.* 2.32), he has Cacciaguida ask "to whom as to you were the gates of heaven twice opened" (*Par.* 15.29–30), to which the only answer is Paul; and when he angrily rejects Filippo Argenti, Virgil says "benedetta colei che'n te s'incinse" (*Inf.* 8.45: "blessed is she who bore you"; cf. the words spoken by a woman in the crowd to Christ after he has

---

[20] The text is from *Cligés*, ed. Alexandre Micha (Paris: H. Champion, 1957).

cast out devils [Luke 11.27]); Cacciaguida addresses him as "O fronde mia in che io compiacemmi" (*Par.* 15.88: "O my branch, in whom I am pleased," as God said of Christ [Matt. 3.17]).

For Dante these analogies are meant to strengthen his message, to make his audience accept him as the spokesman of God. But lyric poets identify themselves with Christ and with other biblical figures for more overtly selfish reasons. In a shameless plea for sympathy, the Archipoeta begins a poem with a play on the Latin hymn "Dies irae": "Fama tuba dante sonum" ("Fame, spreading the sound by trumpet") to summon princes and minstrels to Vienna for the festivities of Reinald the Archchancellor. The hymn reads "Tuba mirum spargens sonum / per sepulchra regionum" ("the trumpet spreading its wondrous sound through the regions of the dead") to summon the souls to judgment before God—a rather extravagant compliment to Reinald, if not to Vienna. Then he turns the poem into a parody of the Jonah story, his own exile and imprisonment compared to Jonah's time in the belly of the whale; the poet, conscious of his sins, fled the Archchancellor as Jonah fled the wrath of God (yet another nod to Reinald). Ruggiero Apugliese, complaining of a false accusation made by his enemies to the bishop and the clergy, reenacts Christ's passion: "Ruggieri à fatto la sua 'Passione' / ... / Erode v'era e Gaifasso / e Pilato ... / e Longino e Giudeasso / ... e Barnabasso" (1.3.21–24: "Ruggieri has suffered his passion ... there were Herod and Caiphas, and Pilate and Longinus and Judas and Barrabas").[21]

The Archipoeta, in a poem which brazenly rehearses his vices in the guise of a plea for mercy (the impressive tour de force of "Estuans intrinsecus"), builds whole parts of the poem with lines from the Bible.[22] But most of the poem is about the poet's

---

[21] More modestly, perhaps, Jacopone, trying to have his excommunication lifted, seeks someone to play Christ to his sinner (2.14.11 ff.). He compares himself to a series of disabled people healed by Christ, the blind of Jericho (Matt. 20.30–34; Mark 10.46–52), the centurion's servant (Matt. 8.6); he lies in the pool at Solomon's gate but no one tells him to get up and take his bed (John 5.4–11).

[22] The first four stanzas begin with echoes of Job 13.25, Matt. 7.234, Sap. 5.10, Ps. 18.11; and three of the last five draw on 2 Cor. 10.15, John

gambling, his desire for women: "meum pectus sauciat puella-
rum decor, / et quas tactu nequeo, saltem corde mechor"; 23–
24: "the beauty of girls wounds my breast, and those I cannot
commit adultery with in the flesh, at least I can in my heart" (a
play on Matt. 5.28: "Ego autem dico vobis, quia omnis, qui
viderit mulierem ad concupiscendum eam, jam moechatus est
eam in corde suo"; "But I say unto you that whosoever looketh
on a woman to lust after her hath committed adultery with her
already in his heart"). And about his drinking: "meum est
propositum in taberna mori, / ut sint vina proxima morientis
ori. / Tunc cantabunt laetius angelorum chori: 'Deus sit propi-
tius huic potatori'"; 44–48: "I propose to die in a tavern, so the
wine will be close to my dying mouth. Then choirs of angels
will sing more happily, 'May God be merciful to this drinker'"
—*potatori*, "drinker," rather than the expected *peccatori*, "sinner."

In "Lingua balbus," the Archipoeta preaches a sermon to the
learned despite his stammering tongue and dull wit ("Lingua
balbus hebes igenio, / viris doctis sermonem facio"). He reminds them that the just judge will inspect our hearts at the
Last Judgment, that since the creator suffered on the cross, he
who does not feel compassion for suffering is iron. As the
divine page testifies, wealth is a burden to the just, charity is
the highest virtue—the poet's direction is clear. He commends
the poor to them, reminding them that the saviour said "Omni
petenti tribue" (33–34: "Give to every man that asketh of thee"
[Luke 6.30]). And finally he gets to the point: "paupertatem
meam non taceo" (st. 36: "I shall not be silent about my poverty"), "nullum decipio / ... nam libenter semper accipio" (st. 3,
"I deceive no one ... freely I receive" [cf. 1 Mach. 9.71; Job
15.34]), "et plus michi quam fratri cupio" ("and I desire more
for me than for my brother"); he goes on to say he would be
ashamed if he had to sell his cloak, a sly reference to "Sell all
that thou hast and give to the poor" [Matt. 20.21], implying that

---

8.7, 1 Reg. 16.7, Eph. 6.9. I have drawn heavily on the work of their
German editors for the biblical references of the Latin poets, here and
elsewhere through the paper.

if they did what Christ preached, he would not have to sell his cloak, his "indumentum varium" (38.2), implying that they are Joseph's evil brothers and he is the innocent victim. He ends praying that God the creator will give them the oil of charity, the wine of hope, the grain of faith, and life after death, while to those of us who are enjoying the world, he will give good wine for frequent drinking, and lots of money for big expenses (44–45).

Even this sort of play with biblical lines is not without its serious side, the implied attacks on clerical corruption. The Bible, the main tool of clerical apologists, moral or political, can be turned against the clergy, by showing either how they abuse it, or how they flout it. In the *Roman de la Rose*, the Bible is employed primarily by shady characters. Papelardie, a figure of clerical hypocrisy, who only appears on the wall of the garden, holds a Psalter (421), and makes himself look thin, as the gospel says hypocrites do (Matt. 6.16), to win praise and vain glory (434–36). Faus Semblant, who "covers his slyness with the mantle of hypocrisy" (11492–94: "j'aim ... affubler ma renardie / du mantel de papelardie") and eventually identifies himself as one of Antichrist's boys (11683), plays a key role in the winning of the rose; he carries a Bible at his neck (12058), peppers his speech with "ce m'a l'Escriture conté" (11300: "so Scripture told me"), and "car l'escriture s'i acorde" (11313: "Scripture agrees on this"), and cites Solomon and Saint Paul in support of his attack on mendicants (though he apparently is one himself [11485–86]). His approach is to forestall argument by suggesting that if you doubt him you slander God: "car Salomon tout a delivre / nous a escrit en un sien livre / de *Paraboles* ... au treintiesme chaspistre / ... ou Dex est menti-erres" (11247–60: "for Solomon wrote it all for us in one of his books, in the thirtieth chapter of Proverbs ... or God is a liar"; cf. 11349: "se del qui fist Adan ne ment"; "if he who made Adam does not lie"). It is indeed Proverbs 30.8–9 that he quotes, though he slips in something of his own about begging.

Faus Semblant boldly cites Matthew against hypocrites:

> que nous lison de saint Maci,
> c'est a savoir l'evangelistre,

ou vint e troisieme chapistre:
"Seur la chaiere Moysi
. . . .
sidrent scribe et pharisien
(ce sunt les fausses genz maudites
que la letre apele ypocrites)"

(11572–80)

for we read in St. Matthew, that is to say the evangelist, in
the twenty third chapter [note the attention to bibliographic
detail]: "On the seat of Moses sat scribes and pharisees,"
these are the false cursed people whom the letter calls
hypocrites.

The other characters in the *Roman* who cite the Bible are Genius
and Nature. Nature, who is God's vicar, knows Faus Semblant
well enough to connect him with the dangerous hypocrites
whom Scripture calls pseudo-prophets (19315–20), but she
accepts his services in her cause and grants him a full pardon.
Genius, who is Nature's priest and a priest of the church (16242
ff.), uses the Bible for verbal attacks on women, their greed,
their duplicity in uncovering men's secrets and gaining control
over them. Then in full regalia as a bishop, wearing a chasuble,
ring, and mitre, and carrying a crozier, he addresses Love's
army, promising them paradise if they do love's work, as if
they were going on a crusade, instead of a rape. That is, he
joins the hypocrites and deceivers in their physical attack on the
woman.

By putting virtually all the biblical material into the mouths
of characters who are working to seduce the rose, Jean de Meun
seems to imply the same sort of point Dante makes explicitly in
the *Comedy*. In *Par.* 29.88 ff., Beatrice speaks of heaven's anger
towards those who distort Scripture, who use it to spin their
own inventions and show off their own cleverness, feeding their
sheep on wind. In Hell, Dante shows the pope, Boniface VIII,
whom he calls the "principe dei nuovi Farisei" (*Inf.* 27.85: "the
prince of the new Pharisees"), using the Bible to help lead a
monk back into sin for his own political needs: "Lo ciel poss'io
serrare e diserrare . . . però son due le chiave" (27.103–4: "I can

open or close heaven ... that is why there are two keys," a reference to Matt. 16.19). By using the keys, he claims, he can absolve Guido of the sin he will commit in his service; Guido in fact allows himself to be misled and therefore never formally repents that sin.

Dante and other poets also invoke the Bible directly to attack clerical corruption, turning it against those who should be preaching and living its message. Walter of Chatillon calls the princes of the church "sellers of spiritual grace, precursors of Antichrist, successors of Judas, who sell Christ today"; referring to Martha and Mary (Luke 10.38–42), figures for the active and contemplative lives, he says Martha is now occupied outside, seeking the grace of gain, while her sister contemplates money, with a pun on *nummus*, "money," and *numen*, "divinity."[23] In "Utar contra vitia," one of the better known poems in the *Carmina Burana*, two plays are made on "give and it shall be given unto you" (Luke 6.38): "dabis aut non dabitur" (7.3: "give or it will not be given") and "si tu michi dederis, ego dabo tibi" (19.4: "if you give to me, I will give to you").

The most impressive example of preaching the Bible against clerics is the gospel according to Saint Silver Mark (CB 44), "Initium sancti evangelii secundum marcas argenti":[24]

In illo tempore: dixit papa Romanis: "Cum venerit filius hominis ad sedem maiestatis nostre, primum dicite 'Amice,

---

[23] "Ecce florent venditores / spiritalis gratie, / Antichristi precursores, / presides ecclesie, / ... tui, Juda, successores, / Christum vendunt hodie / ... Martha foris occupatur / querens lucri gratiam, / soror Marthe contemplatur / nummos et pecuniam" (from "Frigescente caritatis," 12.1 and 3). The text is from *Die Lieder Walters von Chatillon*, ed. Karl Strecker (Berlin: Weidmann, 1925). Cf. passages in the *Carmina Burana*, ed. Alfons Hilka and Otto Schumann (Heidelberg: C. Winter, 1930), vol. 1, Die moralisch-satirischen Dichtungen (hereafter referred to as CB): "Judas Gehennam meruit / quod Christum semel vendidit; / vox autem ... qui septies cotidie / corpus vendunt dominicum / ..." (9.1: "Judas deserved Gehenna because he sold Christ once; you, however, ... who sell the lord's body seven times a day / ...."

[24] For other examples of liturgical parodies, see Franceso Novati, "La parodia sacra nelle letterature moderne," in *Studi critici e letterari* (Turin: Loescher, 1889), 177–266.

ad quid venisti?' At ille si perseveraverit pulsans nil dans vobis, eicite eum in tenebras exteriores." Factum est autem, ut quidam pauper clericus veniret ad curiam domini pape, et exclamavit dicens: "Miseremini mei saltem vos, hostiarii pape, quia manus paupertatis tetigit me. Ego vero egenus et pauper sum, ideo peto ut subveniatis calamitati et miserie mee." Illi autem audientes indignati sunt valde et dixerunt: "Amice, paupertas tua tecum sit in perditione. Vade retro, satanas, quia non sapis ea, que sapiunt nummi. Amen, amen, dico tibi: non intrabis in gaudium domini tui, donec dederis novissimum quadrantem." Pauper vero abiit et vendidit pallium et tunicam et universa que habuit et dedit cardinalibus et hostiariis et camerariis. At illi dixerunt: "Et hoc quid est inter tantos?" Et eiecerunt eum ante fores, et egressus foras flevit amare et non habens consolationem. Postea venit ad curiam quidam clericus dives, incrassatus, impinguatus, dilatatus, qui propter seditionem fecerat homicidium. Hic primo dedit hostiario, secundo camerario, tertio cardinalibus. At illi arbitrati sunt inter eos, quod essent plus accepturi. Audiens autem dominus papa cardinales et ministros plurima dona a clerico accepisse, infirmatus est usque ad mortem. Dives vero misit sibi electuarium aureum et argenteum, et statim sanatus est. Tunc dominus papa ad se vocavit cardinales et ministros et dixit eis: "Fratres, videte, ne aliquis vos seducat inanibus verbis. Exemplum enim do vobis, ut, quemadmodum ego capio, ita et vos capiatis."

Virtually every phrase in this "gospel" comes out of the Bible in a suggestive context, but as they are put together, they deliver a new message:

At that time, the pope said unto the Romans: "When the son of man shall come to the seat of our majesty [Matt. 25.31, on God in judgment], say first: 'Friend, wherefore art thou come?' [what Christ says to Judas in Matt. 26.50]. And if he should continue to knock [Luke 11.8], but give you nothing, cast him into outer darkness" [Matt. 25.30].

The Luke passage goes on to say "Ask and it shall be given

you; seek and ye shall find; knock, and it shall be opened unto you," so the gospel of Silver Mark belies the gospel of Luke. The Matthew passage is from the parable of talents, referring to the unprofitable servant. The "gospel" continues:

And it happened that a certain poor cleric came to the court of the lord pope and cried out, saying "Have pity upon me, O ye door-keepers of the pope for the hand of God hath touched me [Job 19.21]. I am poor and needy [Ps. 69.6], therefore I ask that you succor me in my calamity and misery" [Soph. 1.15]. And when they heard they were moved with indignation [Matt. 20.24; Dan. 14.27] and they said: "Friend, may your poverty be with you unto perdition [Acts 8.20: "Thy *money* perish with thee because thou hast thought that the gift of God can be purchased with money"]. Get thee behind me, Satan, for thou savourest not the things that be of money [Mark 8.33, which speaks of the things of God, not of money]. Amen, amen, I say unto thee: thou shalt not enter into the joy of the lord till thou hast paid the uttermost farthing" [Matt. 5.26, which speaks of deliverance from worldly prisons, not entrance into the joy of the lord]. The poor man went away and sold his cloak and his tunic and all that he had [an inversion of Matt. 19.21: "go and sell that thou hast and give to the poor"] and he gave it to the cardinals and the door-keepers and the chamberlains. But they said: "but what is this among so many?" [John 6.9, said of the loaves and fishes]. And they cast him out [John 9.34], and he went out and wept bitterly [Matt. 26.75] and had not consolation [Lam. 1.9]. And afterwards there came to the court a certain rich cleric, waxen fat, grown thick, covered with fatness [Deut. 32.15], who had committed murder for sedition [Luke 23.19, a reference to Barabbas who was preferred by the populace to Christ]. And he gave first unto the door-keeper, second unto the chamberlain, and third unto the cardinals [Matt. 25.15]. But they thought among themselves that they should have received more [Matt. 20.10, the laborers in the vineyard]. The lord pope, however, hearing that the cardinals and ministers had received many gifts from the cleric, grew sick unto death [Phil. 2.27]. Then the rich man sent him a gold and silver electuary, and immediately he was made whole [John 5.9, the lame man cured after thirty-eight years]. Then the lord pope called unto him the cardinals and ministers and said to them: "Take heed brethren that no man deceive you with vain words [Matt. 24.4; Heb. 3.12.; Eph. 5.6]. For I give you an example, that as I take, so you should take." [John 13.15, where Christ tells the apostles after the washing of feet, to do as he has done; there probably is a pun in *capio*, "take" and "understand"].

I know of no one piece as rich and dense as this, though single examples of the same sort for the same purpose, using the Bible to attack clerical abuses, are scattered through the *Divine Comedy*. *Inferno* 19 and 23, where Dante presents the clerical groups of simoniacs and hypocrites, have a concentration of biblical references which emphasize the souls' willful neglect of the lessons they should have followed and taught. In *Purgatorio* 6 and 16, Dante uses the Bible to sanction his criticism of the church for impeding the empire: "Ahi gente che dovresti esser devota, / e lasciar seder Cesare in la sella, / se bene intendi ciò che Dio ti nota" (6.91–93: "Ah you who ought to be devout and let Cesar sit in the saddle, if you understand what God tells you," a reference to Matt. 22.21, "Render unto Cesar . . ."); and "or discerno perché dal retaggio li figli di Levì furono essenti" (16.131–32: "now I see why the sons of Levi were excluded from the heritage"). In Numbers 18.20–24, the sons of Levi are the priests who serve the tabernacle to whom God says "Thou shalt have no inheritance in their land." In the sphere of justice, Dante decries the buying and selling inside the temple whose walls were built by miracles and martyrdom (18.122–23); and he has St. Peter, the first pope and the one on whom the papacy based many of its claims to power, invoke a series of biblical images to show how far his successors have strayed from Christ's intentions (*Par.* 27). The same images had been used by papalists to claim great powers for the papacy, and particularly by Boniface VIII in the bull *Unam Sanctam*, to which I think this passage is an answer.[25]

In using the Bible to support his political views, particularly the separation of church and state and the denial of temporal power or wealth to the church, Dante is doing nothing unusual, but when he revises the Bible or inserts himself into it as if he were one of God's prophets, he is being fairly bold. He introduces the neutral angels into Hell, although there is only the most tenuous biblical support for them and much doctrine against them, in order to emphasize the importance of taking sides, of making a commitment. In the Earthly Paradise, as he describes the animals in the procession, he tells his audience that he does not have time to give the details but they can read Ezekiel, who is right except about the wings and there "Giovanni è meco e da lui si diparte" (29.105: "John is with me and departs from him"); not "I follow John," but "John is with me." Beatrice tells him he will eventually be a fellow citizen with her of that Rome of which Christ is a *Roman* (32.101–2), a significant addition to Ephesians 2.19: "Now therefore ye are no more strangers and foreigners, but fellow-citizens with the saints and of the household of God"); the citizens become Romans. Beatrice also tells him that the "vessel which the serpent broke was and is not" (33.34–35), applying the phrase which in Revelation refers to the beast (Rev. 17.8)—not to the beast the vessel has become, but to the vessel itself, the church in Dante's poem—to emphasize that the church will not be what it was. Finally, in the most striking gesture of all, Dante joins the procession of the books of the Old and New Testament; since Beatrice will tell him that it is his divine mission to describe what he has seen, Dante is not simply following the Bible, he is carrying on its work, writing what God wants him to write, as if his poem were the third part of the Bible.

Dante may go further in the freedom he takes with the Bible than other poets I have discussed, but he is not unusual in his treatment of it. Normally when secular writers, lay or clerical, used the Bible in their work in the Middle Ages, they did not

---

[25] See *The Political Vision*, 95–96.

hesitate to adapt it to their needs, whether they were preaching morality, attacking corruption, telling stories of heroes or lovers, supporting political figures or causes, seeking something for themselves, or simply trying to amuse or shock the audience. The Bible was indeed a thesaurus from which they could and did draw at will, more often than not to ends very different from those of its holy authors. There were certainly different levels of audience for different kinds of biblical parody; everyone could be expected to know the story of Christ's Passion, the more sophisticated would pick up allusions to the rock on which Christ built his church, only the educated few would catch all the references in the gospel of Silver Mark, but the quantity of such parody suggests its general popularity.

Why there was such freedom with the holy text is another matter. Perhaps the figurative nature of so much biblical language, which forces a certain amount of interpretation, lends itself to parody—if x can stand for y, then why not for z? Perhaps the importance of typology in Christian readings of the Bible—if the Old Testament figures represent someone in later history (Christ), why should they and he not represent still later figures? God's plan, after all, is still unfolding. Indeed, if the whole history told in the Bible and particularly Christ's life and death was all to save me, why should I not use it as I need it? Whatever the reasons, the fact is that the word of God was frequently invoked to embellish and support the word of man, and as often invoked by men of words to attack the men of God who abused God's word.

Prophetic Discourse: St. Augustine to Christine de Pizan

Stephen G. Nichols

Di sùbito drizzato grid ò: "Come?
dicesti 'elli ebbe'? non viv' elli ancora?
non fieri li occhi suoi lo dolce lume?"
Dante. Inf. 10.67–69

Can one reconstruct and criticize a poem other than in a world
of concrete expression and historically reproduced language?
—Antonio Gramsci

I. Augustine's Theory of Mediated Reading

The study of the Bible in the Middle Ages, and particularly
theories of biblical exegesis, have been closely linked to
the master theories for interpreting vernacular literatures from
Early Christian times to the present. Modern trends in this
domain first tended to continue the emphasis on the herme-
neutic theory authorized by the Fathers and their medieval
continuators. In the reaction against historicism and hermeneutics that has marked the post-structuralist period, scholars
have preferred to focus on the language theories of the Fathers,
on their study of the *material* aspects of biblical discourse. As
Eugene Vance has recently observed:

All of Augustine's endeavors in metaphysics, epistemology, and exegesis coincide with a relentless effort to define the functions and limits of human language. Many empirical features of verbal signs, whether pronounced, written, or merely thought, gave rise to analogies that nourished Augustine's speculations about man's relationship to himself, to people and things, and to God.[1]

Vance thus sees Augustine as having inaugurated the "semiological consciousness of the Christian West."[2] Writing from a different viewpoint, G. R. Evans has made equally compelling claims for the role of patristic biblical exegesis in formulating a theory of language communication that would inform the rest of the Middle Ages. In *The Language and Logic of the Bible*, Evans focuses on the patristic consciousness of the linguistic consequences of the Fall as the primordial event determining the context in which expressive forms might be studied:

> The most important effect [of Adam's sin], in the eyes of a number of early Christian writers, was the breakdown of communication between man and God. As Gregory the Great put it in the sixth century, after man was expelled from the joys of paradise and began his exile in this present life in the world, he became blind in his spiritual understanding. . . . It is upon this supposition, that man, through his own fault, is no longer able to understand what God says to him except dimly and imperfectly, that the whole of mediaeval exegesis is founded.[3]

Vance and Evans remind us that the model reading matter in the Middle Ages was the transcendent language of the Bible, but that the *model* of reading was both mediated and theoretical.

---

[1] Eugene Vance, "Saint Augustine: Language as Temporality," in *Mimesis: From Mirror to Method, Augustine to Descartes,* ed. John D. Lyons and Stephen G. Nichols (Hanover: University Press of New England, 1982), 20.

[2] Ibid., 20.

[3] G. R. Evans, *The Language and Logic of the Bible: The Earlier Middle Ages* (Cambridge: Cambridge University Press, 1984), 1.

The opening lines of book 1 of Augustine's *De doctrina christiana* present a theory of reading as a problematic, rigorously intellectualized activity in which Augustine consciously casts himself as mediator, the pedagogue who himself relies on the mediation of the divinity for guidance:

> There are two things necessary to the treatment of Scriptures: a way of discovering those things which are to be understood, and a way of teaching what we have learned. We shall speak first of discovery and second of teaching. This is a great and arduous work, and since it is difficult to sustain, I fear some temerity in undertaking it. It would be thus indeed if I relied on myself alone, but now while the hope of completing such a work lies in Him from whom I have received much concerning these things in thought, it is not to be feared that He will cease giving me more when I have begun to use what He has already given me.[4]

This passage follows the prologue of *De doctrina*, in which Augustine outlines the concept of reading mediated by the dual instruments of the human pedagogue and divine grace. This doubly mediated reading is necessary because the matter of reading, language, cannot be taken as the point of departure, at least not in its purely material form as textuality.

Marcia Colish reminds us that in one of Augustine's first works, the *Soliloquia*, he had formulated the concept of cognition through speech with forceful simplicity:

> Reason: What, then, do you want to know?
> Augustine: The very things for which I have prayed.
> R: Summarize them concisely.
> A: I want to know God and the soul.
> R: Nothing else?
> A: Nothing else at all.[5]

---

[4] *DDC* 1.1.1; Saint Augustine, *On Christian Doctrine*, trans. D. W. Robertson, Jr. (Indianapolis: Bobbs-Merrill, 1958), 7–8.

[5] Augustine, *Soliloquia*, 1.2.7 (*MPL* 32). Quoted by Marcia Colish, *The Mirror of Language: A Study in the Medieval Theory of Knowledge*, rev. ed. (Lincoln: University of Nebraska Press, 1983), 16.

All reading, then, becomes rhetorical reading with divine cognition as its primary goal. In one stroke, Augustine situates a specific epistemology between reader and text. The corollary of this rhetorical theory is the concept of mimetic reading.

In mimetic reading, the object is always the moral status of the reader's subjectivity in relation to divine cognition. The reader will not then read the text, *per se*, but imitate a doctrinally orthodox reading theory, set out in advance to show how the signs in the text are not to be read in and for themselves, but as *signa translata*, "signs of other things."

While it is obvious, on the one hand, what happens to Old Testament language when confronted with this theory of mediated reading, it may be worthwhile to look once more at the fate of Old Testament textuality in books 2 and 3 of *De doctrina*, paying particular attention to the way Augustine handles the language of the prophets. For his authority in this domain had a profound effect on the development of vernacular literature in the early Middle Ages. At the same time, understanding Augustine on prophetic discourse will help us to sort out some fascinating literary innovations in fifteenth-century French literature, particularly in Christine de Pizan's *Ditié de Jehanne d'Arc*.

II. Mediated Reading and Old Testament Textuality

As G. R. Evans observed, "the most important effect of [Adam's sin], in the eyes of a number of early Christian writers, was the breakdown of communication between man and God"; the inability to communicate posed a distinct challenge to their readings of the Old Testament, particularly to their reading of the inspired prophets. For the fact of the matter was that, in terms of the Hebrew Bible, prophecy was a gift, a demonstration of the *divine* and the *human* acting directly in history. The prophetic consciousness, as Abraham Heschel has pointed out, affirmed the proximity of the divine and the human, rather than the distance between the two. The prophets were not so much concerned with a cognitive theory of divinity, as with the problem of witnessing the word of God directly and through their own person.[6]

The prophetic word, from this perspective, is not a mediated word, not a word that conveys "ideas *about* God," but one that "discloses attitudes *of* God."[7] The point here is that the Old Testament viewpoint stresses the materiality of language; the prophet communicates not only directly with God, but engages in a dialogue, which, at least rhetorically, postulates a fellowship or equality of speakers. The understanding of the other, in this dialogue, takes place by direct apprehension of the other's speech. The knowledge of God so obtained is thus not acquired by intellectual processes, such as analogy, metaphor, syllogism, or induction, but directly.

We can see here how Old Testament textuality could offer a clear and present danger to the Augustinian conception of the word. The prophetic consciousness of the Old Testament offered a theory of immanence and direct participation by the reader with God expressed in and through the language of the major prophets. In short, prophetic consciousness offered a direct experience of the text at the literal level and thus a direct participation with a divinity who was not wholly Other. Such a tradition might encourage *commentary*, but not exegesis in the sense developed by Augustine.

We can see the conflict posed by looking at two incidents in Ezekiel that involve corporeal discourse—the use of the flesh as a transcendental signifier. In Ezekiel 2, Yahweh conveys his words to the Jews physically through the body of Ezekiel; he commands Ezekiel to eat the scroll in a direct and unmediated act of carnal identification of logos and being. The purpose of the physical linking of body and word is the purification of corporate society: a dramatic portrayal of its rededication to historical principles, i.e., the covenant.

This is only the beginning of an extended series of corporal metaphors in Ezekiel in which the rebellion of the Israelites is

---

[6] Abraham J. Heschel, *The Prophets. Part II* (New York: Harper & Row, 1962), chapter 1.

[7] Ibid., 1.

likened to carnal defilement. This defilement of the body is a perverse parody of Ezekiel's own literal incorporation of the word in his flesh when he eats the scroll.

Ezekiel clearly distinguishes the spiritual presence of the word *in* the body, and the defilement *of* the body through disobedience. In both cases, the spirit and letter of the law are implicated, with the body as the base metaphor for both literal and figurative expressions. We can thus see how the text of Ezekiel establishes a complex language of corporeal metaphor that is both literal and figurative, historic and transhistoric.

To counter this powerful image of the word which links society and history via the person of the prophet, Augustine substitutes a new conventional system of signs that stress intellectual engagement over the personal, elective, and emotional modes of intuition that mark Ezekiel's language so strongly.

For Augustine, intellectual processes have the advantage of standing between the audience and the phenomenon to be understood: they are lessons rather than illuminations, and thereby subject to control by a pedagogue. Intellectual processes also privilege mentation over intuition and emotion, categories that Augustine ascribes to Old Testament prophetic language, which he explicitly equates with *carnal* discourse—i.e., the use of flesh as a non-transcendent signifier and thus the opposite of what we've just been seeing.

Quoting Ezekiel 36.17–19, Augustine observes:

> It is easy to understand what the prophet Ezekiel said:
> When the house of Israel dwelt in their own land, they defiled it with their ways and their doings; their way was before me like the uncleanness of a menstruous woman. And poured out my indignation upon them for the blood which they had shed upon the land, and with their idols they defiled it.
>
> It is easy, I say, to understand this as it applies to the house of Israel of which the Apostle says, "Behold Israel according to the flesh" [1 Cor. 10.18], because *the carnal people of Israel* did these things.... (*DDC* 3.34.48)

Augustine here exposes what he sees as the impotence of

prophetic language to do more than witness history in one dimension. The prophets cannot be taken as guides, for unmediated, their language simply turns back upon the world. On the other hand, when read as Augustine reads it, the carnal language of the prophets may be transformed into a discourse of the spirit. In other words, Augustine begins, here, to transform not simply the concept of prophetic language, but to substitute, via his critique of it, the *person* of the apostle and saint for that of the prophet; the latter seen as impotent in his prison house of historical language.

For Augustine, emphasizing the materiality of language leads to a "miserable servitude of the spirit . . . so that one is not able to raise *the eye of the mind* above things that are corporeal" (*DDC* 2.5.9). And yet, this was precisely "the servitude of the Jewish people," he says, who

> took signs of spiritual things for the things themselves, not knowing what they referred to, and yet acting as a matter of course as though through this servitude they were pleasing to the One God of All whom they did not see. (*DDC* 3.6.10)

What distinguishes the Christians from the Jews, Augustine argues, is the Christian acceptance of the pedagogue who mediates biblical language for the people. The pedagogue embodies not an experience of the divinity, but a conceptual framework for understanding divine manifestations.

Augustine's exegetical theory, then, envisages a new kind of transformational discourse on a new kind of text, based on a universal doctrine of scriptural intentionality:

> But scripture teaches nothing but charity, nor condemns anything except cupidity, and in this way shapes the minds of men . . . . But scripture asserts nothing except the catholic faith as it pertains to the past, future, and present. *It is a history of past things, an announcement of future things, and an explanation of present things.* (*DDC* 3.10.15)

Let us now turn to the Middle Ages to see how Augustine's substitution of the pedagogue for the prophet can reveal much about the links between biblical exegesis, vernacular narrative poetry, and philosophical anthropology at crucial moments in the evolution of medieval culture.

III. Mediated Reading, Philosophical Anthropology, and Hagiography

The earliest medieval vernacular narrative verse, hagiography, offers a dramatic example of the pedagogical anthropology inaugurated by Augustine. In these saints' lives, indisputably influenced by the Augustinian paradigm of transformation discourse, we find that prophetic language and charismatic vision have been replaced by act and interpretation. Unlike the live prophet, the dead saint offers an inchoate body of legendary deeds that can be shaped at will by the hagiographer. The saint's body of deeds thus offers itself as a virtual text to be completed according to exegetic principles that take his history from the literal or human to the holy or anagogic.

Logically, if unexpectedly, hagiography revalorizes the concept of the body as the locus of meaning, but a meaning that will be displaced away from the corporeal and material. At some point in all hagiography, the Old Testament image of Ezekiel eating the scroll functions as a necessary subtext. But it is a subtext that both fascinates and repels.

Suspicion of the prophetic word led medieval commentators, like Etienne de Bourbon, following the lead of Gregory the Great, to interpret Christ's life as a dual level of communication moving from a didactic and dramatic fleshly expression in the form of deeds to an interpretation that gave the doctrinal meaning of the act:

> (As the blessed Gregory demonstrates in his *Dialogues*, deeds teach more than words, and examples inspire more than exhortations); similarly, Jesus Christ, the *summa* of God's wisdom, taught first by deeds rather than words, and thus he rendered the refinement of preaching pedagogically visible and solidly corporeal, [thereby] investing

and clothing it [doctrine] with diverse figures, parables, miracles, and examples, in order that this doctrine might be grasped more quickly, be understood more easily, be retained in memory more strongly, and thus the whole work be fulfilled more powerfully [*efficacius*].[8]

For Gregory and Etienne de Bourbon, deeds represent a series of expressions linked through the life of the actor—Christ or the *imitatio Christi*. We might think that this notion revives the materiality and historical specificity of the Old Testament prophetic discourse. Just the opposite occurs.

For the deeds which make up the corporeal discourse of the saintly being are only visible signs or signifiers of a pre-existing doctrine simplified for pedagogical purposes. Precisely because they are simplified representations of a hidden and infinitely complex theory—in short, of the "subtlety of preaching" (*subtilitatem predicacionis*)—the naive reader cannot be left to interpret even the simplified examples.

Hagiography thus provides an illustration of the corporeal discourse of the saint as a first step, but then pedagogically leads to the listener/reader through a deconstruction of the corporeal discourse to perceive the true, spiritual meaning of the bodily deeds as "diverse figures, parables, miracles, and examples" (*diversis similitudinibus, parabolis, miracules et exemplis*).

Thus, although the saint, like the prophet, grounds his or her activities in material existence and expression, the expression is never *verbal*, in the first instance, and the saintly mimesis will

---

[8] "magis, ut probat beatus Gregorius in Dyalogorum libro, docent facta quam verba et magis movent exempla quam predicamenta); ideo summa Dei sapiencia, Christus Jhesus, primo docuit factis quam verbis, et subtilitatem predicacionis et doctrine grossam quasi corpoream et visibilem reddidit, muniens et vestiens eam *diversis similitudinibus,* parabolis, miraculis et exemplis, ut ejus doctrina cicius caperetur, facilius cognosceretur, forcius in memoria retineretur et efficacius opere adimpleretur." Stephanus de Borbone, "Prologus, 1," in *Tractatus de Diversis Materiis Praedicabilibus,* in *Anecdotes historiques, légendes, et Apologues tirés du recueil inédit d'Etienne de Bourbon,* publiés par A. Lecoy de la Marche (Paris: Société de l'Histoire de la France, 1877), 4.

transform body to _vita_ as interpreted textuality. Saintly mimesis, always a recapitulation of Christ's already expressed story, thus supplants prophecy by recapitulation.[9]

So in the first two stanzas of the eleventh-century _Vie de saint Alexis_ the clerkly author situates the space of the text away from the historical present in a past where the force of spiritual life measures itself precisely by its ability to transform Old Testament patriarchs into figures of the New.

> Bons fut li secles al tens ancïenur,
> Quer feit i ert e justise ed amur;
> S'i ert creance, dont or n'i at nul prut.
> Tut est müez, perdut ad sa colur:
> Ja mais n'iert tel cum fut as anceisurs.

> Al tens Noë ed al tens Abraham
> Ed al David, qui Deus par amat tant,
> Bons fut li secles; ja mais n'ert si vaillant.

> The world was good in the days of the ancients,
> For justice and love reigned;
> There was faith, no longer prized today.
> All has changed, and lost its freshness:
> Never again will it be as it was for them.

> In the time of Noah, in Abraham's day
> And in David's, whom God loved so much,
> The world was good; never again will it be so worthy.[10]

The pedagogical imperative informing the story to come situates itself in the temporal transformation of the Old Testament patriarchs, the fathers whose bodies are literal signs of the transformational process. Noah, Abraham, and David—the trinitarian configuration indicates how the individual letter or marker yields a collective meaning that transcends the literal context.

Beyond that, Noah, Abraham, and David are patriarchs by virtue of their corporeality, by virtue of the carnality woven into their stories. Noah's carnality, his drunkenness and nakedness—

---

[9] On recapitulation see Augustine, _DDC_ 3.36.52–54.
[10] _La Vie de saint Alexis_, ed. Christopher Storey (Geneva: Droz, 1968).

markers of what Augustine calls "Israel according to the flesh" —makes him a perfect prefiguration of Christ's Passion for Augustine (*DDC* 4.21.45), while for Hugh of Saint Victor, in his *De arca Noe morali*, the ark symbolizes the church and Noah within the ark, Christ in his church.

It is precisely the distance between the literal acts of carnality and the spiritualization of the carnal in Christ's Passion that makes these figures appropriate pedagogical icons for the prologue of the *Alexis*, whose very first independent act and discourse will be a dual renunciation: first of carnal intercourse, then of verbal intercourse.

The typological trinity, Noah, Abraham, and David, can be taken as signs not only of the narrative of transformation, however, but also as markers for the intellectual process generated by the *Alexis*. For by the early Middle Ages, as Hugh of Saint Victor reminds us in his *Didascalicon*, Noah, Abraham, and David were linked to the founding of Near Eastern traditions of learning. They thus stand, at the head of this text, as clerkly signs of the pedagogic imperative redirected, refocused, and unified by Christian doctrine.[11]

Parenthetically, we should note that Hugh, glossing Jerome, also associates David with the demonstration of the distance between carnality and intellect:

> None but Abisag the Sunamite woman warmed the aged David, because the love of wisdom, though the body decay, will not desert her lover. "Almost all the powers of the body are changed in aged men; while wisdom alone increases, all the rest fade away." . . . . The greatness of that love of wisdom, therefore, and the abundance of judgment in elderly men is aptly inferred from the interpretation of that very name "Abisag" which I mentioned above. "For 'Abisag' means 'father mine, superabounding' or again 'my father's deep-voiced cry,' whence it is most abundantly shown that, with the aged, the thunder of divine discourse

---

[11] Hugh of Saint Victor, *Didascalicon*, ed. and trans. Jerome Taylor (New York: Columbia University Press, 1961), book 3, chap. 2, and page 210 n. 34.

tarries beyond human speech. For the word 'superabounding' here signifies fullness, not redundance. And indeed, 'Suna-mitress' in our language means 'scarlet woman,'" an expression which can aptly enough signify zeal for wisdom. (*Didascalicon* 3.14)

The wisdom inculcated by the *Alexis* in the listener comes not from the spoken words of Alexis, after his initial and brief renunciation of even lawful carnal knowledge, but from the gestural language that gradually transforms his life into one of ascesis. The narrative invests the living saint with a series of "diversae similitudines" that mark the different stages of his progress from corporeal to spiritual signifier.

Silence and anonymity characterize his physical existence, the latter part of which takes place in his family's house by way of teaching how even the closest relatives of a saint cannot interpret the grammar of spiritual transformation.

In order to emphasize the dominance of recapitulation over prophecy, the narrative doubles back on itself with a series of overlays at the moment of Alexis's death. The problematic here is not the soul, which flies off on cue:

> tut dreitement en vait en paradis
> A sun seinor qu'il aveit tant servit.
>
> (vv. 333–34)
>
> it goes straight to Paradise,
> To its Lord that it had served so well.

Rather, the text lingers over the body as physical and textual corpus. Alexis's corpse holds the famous *cartre* or letter in which Alexis had set down his life's story. Only a reading of the hagio-autobiography will reveal Alexis's identity, but that reading cannot be performed by the first comer. The body will not release the *cartre* even to Alexis's earthly father.

In a graphic image of the hierarchical nature of mediated reading, the body will only release this *Urtext* of the *vita* to the pope himself. But if the letter can pass directly to the pope, his ecclesiastical rank alone does not authorize him to read it or even examine it. Like us, he too requires a pedagogue for reading. That office can only be performed by "a good and learned clerk."

Li apostolie tent sa main a la cartre;
Sainz Alexis la sue li alascet:
Lui le consent ki de Rome esteit pape.
Il ne la list ne il dedenz ne guardet:
Avant la tent ad un boen clerc e savie.

(75.371–75)

The Apostle holds out his hand to the letter;
Saint Alexis releases his to him;
He consents this to him who was pope of Rome.
(The pope) neither reads nor looks within it:
but gives it first to a good and learned clerk.

The essence of the saint, then, lies in deferred identity and hierarchically conferred status. Unlike the prophet, who is both chosen and self-proclaimed, and whose identity derives from the prophetic discourse spoken during his lifetime, the life of the saint is largely a posthumous elaboration; an interpolation by an authoritative reader for an audience of the faithful who are to be instructed and edified. Even in his own *vita*, Alexis cannot receive the epithet *sainz* until the moment of his death.

The basic lesson of hagiographic textuality is the dual problematic of the present life and corporeality. The only good body, in a sense, is a dead body, a body that can become a *signum translatum*. This means not prophecy of things to come in the world, but a recapitulation of "those things which are before." Hence, despite appearances, the hagiographic text defers closure.

Just as the *vita* really begins with the death of the saint's body, so the meaning of the saint's life begins with the body of posthumous works inspired by the dual corpus, the body as relic(s) and the body as text or *vita*. The presence of these dual signifiers continues to feed the legend of the saint as relics and texts provoke further "diverse signs and miracles" among the faithful. These accretions to the saintly legend are, of course, recapitulations of the already told story descending down in time to the historical present. The power of the saint, therefore, lies in its potency to continue to demonstrate, recapitulatively, the dominance of the patristic paradigm over the prophetic consciousness.

IV. Christine de Pizan and the
Renewal of Prophetic Discourse

The *Alexis* stands, Janus-faced, on the dividing line between two cultures. By its insistence on the mimetic incorporation of Christian doctrine in the person of the pedagogue and exemplary being (saint) it looks *back* to the early phase of Christian intellectualism dominated by the Augustinian model. By its layered textuality, and its implicit demonstration of textual communities, the *Alexis* looks *forward* to what Brian Stock has recently described as a new socialization of knowledge; a socialization of knowledge that produced deep changes in the learned disciplines and thus in the range and conception of biblical hermeneutics.

Thanks to the ever-increasing availability of texts, Stock argues, a new relationship developed between scholars and their material. Knowledge now came to be accepted as an abstract body, too great to be assimilated by any one person:

> A difference was recognized between the knower as inquiring subject and the knowledge which was to be the object of his investigations. Unlike the eastern "wise man" and the early medieval sage, the twelfth-century intellectual did not *embody a subject personally*: he taught it. Being an intellectual was a profession, even a social role.[12]

This fact allowed the Old Testament to be viewed much more objectively than previously. It allowed Hugh of Saint Victor, for example, to return to the *letter* of the Old Testament, precisely to that aspect stigmatized by Augustine as "corporeal language." And it is on the corporeality, the material and historical nature of the Old Testament, that Hugh focuses, even to the point of "visualizing the scene" as he does in his *De arca Noe morali*.[13]

---

[12] Brian Stock, *The Implications of Literacy: Written Language and Models of Interpretation in the Eleventh and Twelfth Centuries* (Princeton: Princeton University Press, 1983), 328.

[13] See Beryl Smalley, *The Study of the Bible in the Middle Ages* (Notre Dame, IN: University of Notre Dame Press, 1964), 96–97.

As Beryl Smalley has written, "Hugh's exegesis conforms to his ideas" on the importance of the literal in the Old Testament.[14] He focused not on the canonical apostolic texts, but rather commented on the literal sense of major Old Testament books, including the prophets.

In Hugh, we find the first attempts to understand the prophetic idiom as a language grounded in the materiality of history and in the person of the prophet as a being with a special relationship to God. In short, he restores the concept of textual intentionality to prophetic discourse, as we may see in this passage from his commentary on the prologue to Joel:

That which is said: *The word of the Lord came to Joel:* signifies in its spiritual sense that the fulfillment of the prophecy which follows belongs chiefly to the Incarnation of the Word [on account of the mystical meaning of *Joel* and *Phatuel*]. It can be understood *more correctly*, however, as referring to the siege and depopulation of the city and territory of Joel, when the town was besieged by the Assyrians under Senacherib, the land laid waste, the aspect of people and country, by the magnitude of the disaster wholly changed.[15]

What we begin to see in Hugh and his successors is the concept of allegorical interpretation being replaced by the analogical method in exegesis. Allegory, as Augustine showed, privileges substitution; it denies or suppresses the difference of the original text, thereby introducing a major asymmetry between the two parts of the equation.[16] Analogy, however,

---

[14] Smalley, 97.

[15] Quoted in Smalley, 101.

[16] In the power of allegory to read disparates as similarities lay its strength as an exegetical method for demonstrating the unity of the Bible as A. J. Minnis has noted in *Medieval Theory of Authorship: Scholastic Literary Attitudes in the Later Middle Ages* (London: Scolar Press, 1984), 46:

The exegetical method whereby the unity of the Bible was established was allegory.... As described in the *Glossa ordinaria* and in other commentaries, the *materia* of the Psalter is not—as is usually the case with the *materia* of a secular work—the subject-matter

allows both elements in a comparison to retain their properties of difference while still permitting the evocation of similarities. Allegory in the Middle Ages tended to fall under the concept of *translatio*, whereby, as we saw in the example of the *Alexis*, the saint replaces the prophet. In the case of analogy, one need not think in terms of substituting one category for the other.

In the sense I want to use it here, analogy is a semiotics of spatializing thought that allows a proposition in one order to inform and shape meanings in another while permitting both to maintain their separate identities or differences. Analogy of this sort generates *identities grounded in space and time that interrogate one another.* Applied to the question of prophetic identity in the late Middle Ages, the new system of analogical exegesis moves away from the concept of saint to envisage a new kind of Christian prophet who fulfills an analogous social, historical, and theological role to that of the Old Testament prophet.

This is exactly what one finds in a fascinating and largely misunderstood work by Christine de Pizan, the *Ditié de Jehanne d'Arc*.[17] Completed on July 31, 1429, this poem of sixty-one stanzas and 488 lines is the last work of Christine's that we possess, if not the last she wrote. It was the first to have been composed on Joan and the only one written during her lifetime.[18]

---

understood literally, but rather its central allegorical referent, the whole Christ. Similarly, the heading *intentio* introduces a statement about allegorical sense rather than literal sense.

Similarly, allegory permitted the dehistoricization of textual referentiality. Allegorical readings of Virgil's *Aeneid*, like that of Bernardus Silvestris on the ekphrastic portraits of the Temple of Juno in Carthage, *Aeneid* 1, for example, freed the Virgilian text from historical contextualization, enabling it to serve, among other things, as a subtext for Guillaume de Lorris's ekphrastic portraits on the wall of the Jardin de Déduit in the *Roman de la rose*. See my article, "Ekphrasis, Allegory, Iconoclasm: Virgil and the *Roman de la rose*," in *Rethinking the "Romance of the Rose"*, ed. Kevin Brownlee and Sylvia Hunt (forthcoming).

[17] Christine de Pizan, *Ditié de Jehanne d'Arc*, ed. Angus J. Kennedy and Kenneth Varty, Medium Aevum Monographs, new series, 9 (Oxford: Society for the Study of Medieval Languages and Literature, 1977).

[18] *Ditié*, 1.

The *Ditié* has not been treated as hagiography, nor did Christine make that claim herself—as the title indicates (Joan's canonization being still some 491 years distant [1920] in 1429). And yet Christine consistently utilizes categories of the sacred, both prophetic and hagiographic, to celebrate this yet living "miracle," this "Pucelle eslite," "Pucelle beneurée," and

> Pucelle de Dieu ordonnée,
> En qui le Saint Esprit réa
> Sa grant grace. . . .

> (171–73)

Maiden sent from God, into whom the Holy Spirit poured his great grace.

Very briefly, the poem situates itself at the apogée of Joan's triumph: Orleans taken from the English, Charles crowned at Rheims, and Paris expected to be liberated very soon. Christine evokes her own situation of enforced exile briefly, celebrates the king—"Or faisons feste à nostre roy!"—at greater length, then, in stanza 21, she turns definitively to Joan's story. She does not "tell the story," however, in any straightforward way, although most of the facts as we know them appear. Instead, she makes Joan into an artefact, a text, to be studied and glossed in a number of different ways.

Joan or her deeds become the focus of a series of apostrophes, direct addresses—to Joan, to the French people, to the English— each one of which transforms Joan into a different "idiom." In effect, these passages are Christine's assertion that Joan, like all great and sacred beings, is a symbolic form whose greatness can be measured by the multiple ideolects she can assume. Thus, she may be "spoken" as New Testament or Old Testament discourse; she may be cast as prophecy; as vision; as history; and as ritual—we find, for example, the evocation of Joan's guiding presence at Charles's coronation in Rheims twelve days before Christine composed the *Ditié*. Finally, she can be cast in the subjunctive mode of futurity as Christine speculates on the impending liberation of Paris.

Each of these discursive strategies provides Joan with a different identity and genealogy. Christine sees her as announced by history but, also, at every turn, as somehow differing from the precedents to which she is analogous. Thus, in the very first discursive space devoted to Joan, from stanzas 21–25, Christine sets up a textual and doctrinal genealogy based on the Old and New Testaments. Boldly, in the space of one stanza Christine postulates an earthly Trinity that may be seen as a *manifestatio* of the celestial Trinity with the important difference that in earthly trinitarian order the daughter replaces the son:

> Tu, Jehanne, de bonne heure née,
> Benoist soit cil qui te créa!
> Pucelle de Dieu ordonnée,
> En qui le Saint Esprit réa
> Sa grant grace, en qui ot et a
> Toute largesse de hault don,
> N'onc requeste ne te véa.
> Qui te rendra assez guerdon?
>
> (22.169–76)

> You, Joan, born at a propitious moment,
> Blessed be He who created you!
> Maiden sent from God,
> Into whom the Holy Spirit poured
> His great grace, in whom there was and is
> An abundance of noble gifts,
> Never did He deny you any request.
> Who can ever reward you sufficiently?

In keeping with the synoptic nature of soteriological time, Christine contains this identifying movement within a single, highly compressed stanza, in which the two orders virtually superimpose themselves one on the other. But the mystical union grounds itself in historical pragmatics. Joan's trinitarian identity links Joan and France to providential intention via the New Testament:

> Puis que Dieu t'a tant honnorée
> Que as la corde desliée
> Qui tenoit France estroit liée. . . .
>
> (21.163–65)

> Since God honored you so greatly
> That you untied the rope

That held France so tightly bound. . . .

Christine next establishes the same pragmatic link between Joan, France, and the Old Testament. In the two opening sequences, Christine had already placed early fifteenth-century France under the sign of Exodus. Now she introduces the figures of Moses and Joshua. In keeping with the Chronological mode of the Pentateuch and historical books, the text proceeds sequentially to work out the complexities of Joan's Old Testament identity in successive stanzas. Christine thus replicates in her own text the temporal distinction between Old and New Testaments.

The Old Testament stanzas of the *Ditié* do not simply establish an analogical equation between Joan and the patriarchal figures; they problematize the analogy even as they posit it. Past and present coexist dialectically; the authority of the past confers aura on the present, but the present, in the person of Joan, forces a re-reading, a re-evaluation of the past.

Moses led the "people of God" from Egypt, Joan simply led "nous," us, out of evil: the imperious claims of the litotes, "nous," are eloquent. Moses led the people to freedom and gave them the law; Joan frees them and offers them her breast as sustenance. Moses stood in the patriarchal image of God, but Joan's identity has no precedent. It overlays the patriarchal and heroic image that her deeds evoke with a series of contradictory ones: virgin/mother; daughter/soldier; peasant/leader; historical prophet/contemporary figure.

Contradiction thus marks Joan's identities: contradiction and rule violation or unnaturalness. One can easily parse the patriarchal grammar of the Old Testament figures, but to construe Joan's grammar there are no rules: Joan is "a phenomenon beyond nature" ("Véez bien chose oultre nature!" [v. 192]).

By separating the Moses and Joshua analogies into two stanzas, and by intercalating one devoted entirely to Joan between the other two, Christine clearly demonstrates that Joan incarnates in her single being the functions accorded to two patriarchal figures. This suggests, in turn, that the contradictory emblems of sword and breast that identify her denote, in effect, a new category of the sacred and a new kind of scripture that like its subject "has a heart greater than any man's":

> Mais ce fait Dieu, qui la conseille,
> En qui cuer plus que d'omme a mis.
>
> (26.207–8)

This is God's doing: it is He who counsels her,
And placed within her a heart greater than any man's.

The *Ditié* continues by making Joan the messianic subject of classical, patristic, and celtic prophecy: the Sybil, Bede, and Merlin, all, at various times, foretold her coming. The coronation scene at Rheims is thus an *avènement* in the double sense of Charles's accession to the throne and the "accession to history" or realization of the prophecies. Historical discourse and historical event come together in the person of this prophet who reunites the secular and sacred in a new harmony:

> En Christianté et l'Eglise
> Sera par elle mis concorde.
> Les mescreans dont on devise,
> Et les herites de vie orde
> Destruira, car ainsi l'acorde
> Prophecie, qui l'a predit,
> Ne point n'aura misericorde
> De lieu, qui la foy Dieu laidit.
>
> (42.329–36)

To Christendom and the Church
She will restore harmony.
The evil doers we've been talking about,
And the heretics with their filthy lives
She will all destroy, for so it has been decreed
By prophecy, which predicted her,
Nor will she have mercy
On any place which treats faith in God with disrespect.

Joan's portrayal as the *avènement* in French history of a lost tradition of prophecy, brings us, as a final point, to the whole question of the prophetic signature of this work. If Joan is the prophet-figure, Christine's is the prophetic voice and the vision. Indeed, within the space of the text, Christine's voice and her situation command our attention from the outset.

> Je, Christine, qui ay plouré

> XI and en abbaye close,
> Où j'ay toujours puis demouré
> Que Charles (C'est estrange chose!)
> Le filz du roy, se dire l'ose,
> S'en fouÿ de Paris de tire,
> Par la traïson là enclose,
> Ore à prime me prens à rire.

(vv. 1–8)

I, Christine, who have wept for eleven years in a walled
abbey
where I have lived ever since
Charles (how strange this is!)
the King's son—dare I say it—?
fled in haste from Paris,
I who have lived enclosed there on account of the treachery,
now, for the first time, begin to laugh.

We sense here a poetic identity poles apart from the clerkly
pedagogue who mediates our reading of the *Alexis*. Christine
inserts herself not simply as an active voice, but as a being who
traces in her own body, in her emotional and physical existence,
the recent history of the political polity of France: its exile,
suffering, and lamentation.

By embodying the diaspora of the French court and the
powerlessness of its leader, Christine assumes the authority of
a collective voice, a subjectivity grounded in national identity.
At the same time, the *Ditié* couples this sense of national identity with a reaffirmation of a covenant with Providence for which
Joan and her victories are the sign. In other words, in yet
another reversal or overlay of traditional Judeo-Christian sym-
bolism, Christine makes Joan the feminine sign of the new
covenant between God and the French, replacing, in yet another
contradiction, the circumcision as the old sign of the covenant.

> Si croy fermement que tel grace
> Ne te seroit *de Dieu donnée*,
> Se à toy, en temps et espace,
> Il n'estoit de Lui ordonnée
> Quelque grant chose solempnée
> A terminer et mettre à chief,

> Et qu'il t'ait donnée destinée
> D'estre de tresgrans faiz le chief.
>
> (vv. 113–20)

And I firmly believe that God would never have bestowed such grace upon you if it were not ordained by Him that you should, in time and space, accomplish and bring to completion some great and solemn task; I believe, too, that He has destined you to be the author of very great deeds.

Now in announcing the regeneration of the French in this way, Christine imprints her work with a prophetic signature. For the prophet, as Claude Tresmontant points out in his book, *Le prophétisme Hébreu*, takes as her task the revelation of divine providence working in history in collaboration with humans.[19]

As mediator of the divine word, the prophet witnesses directly by participating in the generative or regenerative message. Prophetic discourse is thus corporeal in the sense that the prophet embodies the divine language in historical space and time. And the message, as we saw earlier, always conveys the collaborative experience of providence in human affairs. The message embodied by the prophet demonstrates the affective involvement of Providence with the collectivity, with the national polity as a whole.

Thus whereas hagiography of the early Middle Ages avoids contemporary history and politics, prophetic discourse engages them. And Christine takes as her divinely assisted task the revelation of the renewal of providential participation in the rebirth of French political fortune:

> Mais or vueil raconter comment

---

[19] "Le prophète est un homme créé par Dieu pour cet office, la communication à l'humanité, en cette zone germinal ou embryonnaire qui est le peuple hébreu, de l'information créatrice qui vient de Dieu.... Le messager de dieu ... dans beaucoup de [textes] de la bibliothèque hébraïque, c'est dieu lui-même qui se manifest. Ce n'est pas un être autre que Dieu.... Le prophète hébreu est celui à qui Dieu communique un message, une connaissance, une information afin que celui-ci les communique entre Dieu et l'Homme. Il est bien évidemment homme lui-même, mais il est l'homme de l'Esprit, *ha-nnabi ... isch ha-ruach* (Osée, 9, 7)." *Le prophétisme Hébreu* (Paris: J. Gabalda, 1982), 19, 21, 23.

> Dieu a tout ce fait de sa grace,
> A qui je pri qu'avisement
> Me doint, que rein je n'y trespasse,
> Raconté soit en toute place,
> Car c'est digne de memoire,
> Et escript, à qui que desplace,
> En mainte cronique et hystoire!

> (49–56)

But now I wish to relate how God, to whom I pray for guidance lest I omit anything, accomplished all this through His grace. May it be told everywhere, for it is worthy of being remembered, and may it be written down—no matter whom it may displease—in many a chronicle and history-book!

Christine does not attempt to occupy or parallel the prophetic space of the Old Testament—no more than she attempts to displace it in the Augustinian manner. Instead, she evokes it continually as dialogical voice of otherness that exists simultaneously within the text, as we have seen, alongside New Testament and Old French allusions and subtexts. Christine simply takes the traditional exegetical concept of three- and four-fold meaning and collapses it into a new dimension of textual space/time that tolerates, and indeed solicits, multiple typification.

Although traditional exegetical meaning levels were spatially superimposed within the same verbal structures, their meaning was temporally progressive. As we have seen, mediated reading required an escalated ascent through meanings from the literal to the anagogic. Reading was thus a mimesis of the spiritual movement out of the world and beyond language—the "tolle lege" model.

Christine's text, however, recaptures something of the materiality of Old Testament prophetic language with its presumption of providential immanence. In effect, she offers a new version of the traditional exegetical system but, in her case, with temporally and spatially simultaneous meaning levels. Her language, in other words, forms a space/time continuum in which superimposed images remain grounded and active at all levels of meaning production. We proceed through the text not to transcend it or transform it, but to come back continually to the information it reveals.

The crucial difference between her "hagiography" and that of the *Alexis*, for example, is that we do not "progress" from one level of meaning to the other. Each remains, reads, and informs the others continuously. The spiritual category of "saint" attained by Alexis, after his death, at the end of the work, indicates the distance he and the reader have travelled from the material world of carnality portrayed at the beginning. On the other hand, the opposite is true of Joan. Christine continually returns to Joan's original status as "femme" and "bergère," woman, peasant, shepherdess, even when recounting her glory. Revelation, unlike transformation, turns on the fulcrum of recognizing difference.

In closing, I shall give one more example of how Christine analogizes her prophetic discourse to that of the Old Testament without either appropriating or displacing it. The first four stanzas of the *Ditié*, particularly 3 and 4, offer an image of a sympathetic blending of the poet's biological cycle with the seasonal cycle. In this opening, Christine draws upon a well-known convention of the medieval lyric, in general, and, in particular, on Guillaume de Machaut's transformation of the *dit* from a rather uninspiring genre to a complex instrument of poetic expression and self-identity. This initial movement, recalling the indigenous heritage of her poetic language and form, reminds us that Christine grounds her own voice and the identity of her subject, Joan, firmly in a vernacular heritage, that is, France in both the linguistic and popular sense. Furthermore, the *dit* may be connected historically with an early-medieval form of short poetic narrative (also octosyllabic, like Christine's *ditié*) which Marie de France, the first French woman poet, re-created from a popular oral genre.

Poetic convention, especially in the Old French tradition, almost always turns out to be deceptive in its apparent simplicity. So it proves here. Christine provides markers that sooner or later oblige us to recognize that under the vernacular mode of textuality lies a network of Old Testament subtexts.

In fact, the opening of Christine's *Ditié* must be read back onto such prophetic texts as the opening of "The Book of the Consolation of Israel" in Isaiah 40. Christine herself tells us that she has spent eleven years "en abbaye close." Besides lamenting the fate of France and the King, she certainly read Scripture, and Isaiah 40 is the locus of the famous prophecies of the coming of the Messiah:

40.3 The voice of him that crieth in the wilderness, Prepare ye the way of the Lord, make straight in the desert a highway for our God.

40.4 Every valley shall be exalted, and every mountain made low: and the crooked shall be made straight, and the rough places, plain:

40.5 And the glory of the Lord shall be revealed, and all flesh shall see it together: for the mouth of the Lord hath spoken it.

Now Christine does not begin the *Ditié* by announcing the victories of Joan or the coronation of Charles, as we might expect. She begins, in the first person, by announcing to the French people the end of eleven years of exile and lamentation, and (later) the imminent end of the war. Similarly, Isaiah 40 opens when the prophet is commanded to speak to the people:

40.1 Speak ye comfortably to Jerusalem, and cry unto her, that her warfare is accomplished, that her iniquity is pardoned: for she has received of the Lord's hand double for all her sins.

But it is not just in the opening stanza that Christine announces the end of French servitude. The conventional opening description of nature puts the same idea in terms of mutability, in terms of the vulnerability of human life to natural cycles. In this case, Christine makes the allegorical sun in stanza 3 and poetic language itself instruments of providence capable of withering or renewing life. The equations that Christine makes allusively, but concretely, may be found spelled out stridently in the text of Isaiah 40.6-8:

40.7 The grass witherith, the flower fadeth: because the spirit of the Lord bloweth upon it: Surely the people is grass.

This image of the creative breath of providence introduces a key section of the work, the "Prophecy of the Theophany," with its famous vision of Yahweh "coming with his power," as the great shepherd:

40.10 Here is the Lord Yahweh coming with power, his arm subduing all things to him. The prize of his victory is with him, his trophies all go before him.

40.11 He is like a shepherd feeding his flock, gathering lambs in his arms, holding them against his breast. . . .

Isaiah is a rich text, and one readily finds other passages that, when read dialogically with Christine's, tell us much about her reading of Isaiah as analogue for her revelation of Joan as a prophet and messiah figure. As one final item, consider this superposed image of sword and word in the mouth of the prophet; it comes, not coincidentally, I think, from the section of Isaiah that prophecies the restoration of Zion:

49.1 Yahweh called me before I was born. From my mother's womb he pronounced my name.

49.2 He made my mouth a sharp sword, and hid me in the shadow of his hand. He made me into a sharpened arrow, and concealed me in his quiver.

49.3 He said to me, you are my servant (Israel) in whom I shall be glorified.

This simultaneous image of the sword in the mouth might serve as an icon of Christine's *Ditié* with its concept of corporeal discourse; an icon of its proximity to and distance from the Scripture it evokes in almost every stanza. For with this image, we have come full circle. Augustine's paradigm of mediated reading took vernacular literature away from the present and ultimately out of history, with such genres as hagiography, the *chansons de geste*, and the *roman d'antiquité*. Christine, however, by revalorizing the alterity of the Old Testament, situates herself and her poetry in the mainstream of contemporary history. Prophetic discourse becomes, in her hands, an instrument for revealing the agonistic face of history in opposition to its own past.

Pictorial Emphases
in Early Biblical Manuscripts

Robert G. Calkins

The development of pictorial narrative in Early Christian through Romanesque manuscripts has been widely studied and has been dominated by iconographical analyses of unusual scenes and investigations of stylistic characteristics.[1] Normally the narrative scenes in these manuscripts are traced back to lost Early Christian prototypes, best reflected by fragments of the largely destroyed Cotton Genesis in the British Library,[2] or related to a variety of extra-biblical texts. But as important as these iconographical, stylistic, compositional, and textual studies of the narrative illustrations in early medieval Bibles have been, another significant avenue of analysis, intrinsic to the nature of the book, should also be investigated: the creation of a meaningful or programmatic statement achieved through either decorative or pictorial emphasis. Although this paper will concentrate on what appears to be such a statement in the Lambeth Bible in London, particularly through an emphasis on the Book of Daniel, and its reflection of larger didactic

---

[1] For an overview of the state of the question, see R. Kozody, "The Origins of Early Christian Book Illustration," *Gesta* 10 (1971): 33–40.

[2] MS. Cotton Otho B VI: see W. R. Lethaby, "The Painted Book of Genesis in the British Museum," *Archeological Journal* 69 (1912): 88 ff.; K. Weitzmann, "Observations on the Cotton Genesis Fragments," in *Late Classical and Medieval Studies in Honor of Albert Mathias Friend, Jr.*, ed. K. Weitzmann (Princeton, 1955), 112 ff.; idem, *Late Antique and Early Christian Book Illumination* (New York, 1977), 72–75; and most recently, K. Weitzmann and H. Kessler, *The Cotton Genesis; British Library Codes Cotton Otho B. VI* (Princeton, 1986).

and Apocalyptic themes, a preliminary explanation of the background of choices from which such emphasis was derived is in order.

It is possible to differentiate in early biblical manuscripts two parallel traditions of illustration. The first is a tradition of copiously expanded pictorial narration. The second involves the use of a single miniature to introduce a volume, individual books of the Bible, or groups of books, usually a frontispiece; and this gives rise to the necessity to select one or a few incidents to summarize the contents of the specific text. Essentially the latter tradition is a synoptic mode of illustration, which, while more restricted, makes possible a didactic or programmatic selection or juxtaposition of images that go beyond a mere narrative function.[3] A didactic or programmatic statement may also result from a series of pictorial images (usually miniature pages) or even from a sequence of purely decorative elements (ornamental, foliate, or even embellished title pages) that build cumulatively toward either a decorative crescendo or an unfolding of a focused narrative. Such a sequence reveals itself as one turns pages of an illuminated manuscript, building on successive visual impressions to create a memory of additive images that adds up to a "program" or statement that is larger than the mere sum of individual ornamental or miniature pages.[4] Out of these sequential possibilities an effect of an *emphasis* on a specific, focused narrative can result from the

---

[3] Some scholarly attention has been paid to Bibles decorated in this manner, notably by Wilhelm Köhler and Herbert Kessler in their studies of the frontispieces in Carolingian Bibles, and Peter Brieger in a discussion of the early Romanesque St. Vaast Bible: W. Köhler, *Die Karolingischen Miniaturen*, 1, *Die Schule von Tours*, 3 vols (Berlin, 1930–33), 2:193–212; summarized in C. R. Dodwell, *Painting in Europe 800 to 1200* (Harmondsworth, 1971), 35; H. Kessler, *Illustrated Bibles from Tours* (Princeton, 1977); P. H. Brieger, "Bible Illustration and Gregorian Reform," *Studies in Church History* 2 (1965): 154–55.

[4] This theme is developed in R. G. Calkins, "The Golden Age of Imperial Illumination," in *Programs of Medieval Illumination*, The Franklin D. Murphy Lectures 5, Helen Foresman Spencer Museum of Art, University of Kansas (Lawrence, 1984), 8–111, and idem, "Liturgical Sequence and Decorative Crescendo in the Drogo Sacramentary," *Gesta* 25 (1986): 19–27.

selection, frequency, or even omission of images, as well as their placement and relationship to the structure of the manuscript. The nature of these traditions, although often heavily intertwined with each other, comes into focus as one tries to arrive at an understanding of the choices of decoration in these books.

The use of expanded narrative cycles, as Weitzmann has shown, is strongly based on a classical tradition of narrative illustrations of scrolls.[5] These illustrations were inserted into columns of text near the appropriate passage, and this device was then adapted to Early Christian codices. The Quedlinburg Itala fragment in East Berlin, the earliest surviving example of an illustrated biblical book, now consists of only a few leaves, with four framed scenes within a single unifying frame, but originally it was a luxuriously illustrated Book of Kings that may have had as many as sixty full-page miniatures containing two to three hundred individual scenes.[6] The Cotton Genesis of the fifth or sixth century, now a charred fragment in the British Library from which only a few watercolor copies had been made before its destruction, contained about 330 miniatures, presenting an almost cinematic sequence of illustrations expanding a single episode into a number of successive scenes.[7] The sixth-century Vienna Genesis manifested a more rigorous structure, with text appearing on the top half of the folios and miniatures on the bottom half (fig. 1).[8] Only a fragment now, it may have contained originally as many as ninety-six folios.[9] Since many miniatures contained more than one incident, this manuscript may have been even more copiously illustrated than the Cotton Genesis. All of these manuscripts are believed to

---

[5] K. Weitzmann, *Illustrations in Roll and Codex: A Study of the Origins and Method of Text Illustration*, Studies in Manuscript Illumination 2, 2d ed. (Princeton, 1970). See also the important review by H. Bober in the *Art Bulletin* 30 (1948): 284–88.

[6] Inabel Lavin, *The Quedlinburg Itala Fragments*, Letterae textuales (Leiden, 1986); K. Weitzmann, *Late Antique and Early Christian Book Illumination* (New York, 1977), 15, 40.

[7] Ibid., 15–16, 72–75; see also note 2 above.

[8] See Weitzmann's reconstruction, *Roll and Codex*, figures D and E, 90 and 92, for a codex prototype for the Vienna Genesis.

[9] Weitzmann, *Late Antique*, 16, 76–87.

Fig. 1. Vienna, Österreichische Nationalbibliothek, Cod. Theol. gr. 31, Vienna Genesis, fol. 16r. Joseph and Potiphar's Wife.

have been single books of the Bible that were bound individual-
ly.

There were also extensively illustrated volumes containing
groups of the biblical books, the Pentateuch, Hexateuch, Octa-
teuch or the Gospels in which the miniatures were set into the
text. The seventh-century Ashburnham Pentateuch, now in
Paris, may have had sixty-nine full or partial-page miniatures
(only eighteen remain), many with multiple scenes: as for
example, the full-page miniature depicting Adam and Eve after
the Fall and Cain and Abel in the text of Genesis (fig. 2).[10] The
incidents to be illustrated usually reinforce the narrative of the
text, although one often finds extraneous details derived from
Apocryphal books or exegetical commentaries, or even from the
illuminator's imagination. In all of these illustrated volumes we
have series, or cycles of miniatures derived from a variety of
sources—perhaps Early Christian frescoes or mosaics as found
in Early Christian basilicas or, for that matter, in a third-century
Jewish temple at Dura Europas, or even extra-biblical Judaic
sources.[11] Regardless of the variation of individual scenes, or
the introduction of unusual iconographical motifs, the emphasis
is on a pictorial elaboration of the narrative that parallels,
reinforces, expands, and comments on that of the text.

To provide this kind of extended pictorial amplification in a
one-volume Bible, however, presents a major problem. A full
length Bible in one volume (or pandect) is physically a thick,
heavy book to start with, and to add countless additional folios
for narrative miniatures would make it unmanageable. Various
alternatives were therefore developed, and these result in the
second, synoptic tradition mentioned above. One option was to
restrict the decoration or miniature to the opening of each book
according to a hierarchy of ornament, and indeed we find this
device in many medieval Bibles. A book might begin with a

---

[10] O. von Gebhard, *The Miniatures of the Ashburnham Pentateuch*
(London, 1883); Weitzmann, *Late Antique*, 17, 118–25.

[11] B. Narkiss, "Towards a Further Study of the Ashburnham Penta-
teuch," *Cahiers Archéologiques* 19 (1969): 45 ff.; J. Gutmann, "The Jewish
Origin of the Ashburnham Pentateuch Miniatures," *Jewish Quarterly
Review* 44 (1953): 53 ff.

Fig. 2. Paris, Bibliothèque Nationale, MS. n.a. lat. 2334, Ashburnham Pentateuch, fol. 6r. Adam and Eve after the Fall, Cain and Abel.

major decoration, a decorative (probably foliate) or historiated (containing a pictorial scene) initial, or a miniature; and its preface or *Argumentum* usually would be introduced by an initial of lesser visual impact, often a smaller decorative letter. Theoretically, miniatures might be placed before each of these books, but some books of the Bible, particularly those of the Law and the Epistles, do not lend themselves to pictorial narration. One solution, used in a Syriac Bible now in Paris (Bibliothèque Nationale, MS. syr. 341), believed to have been made in Mesopotamia in the sixth or seventh century, contains column-wide miniatures for the most part depicting standing portraits of the authors, heroes, prophets, or evangelists.[12] Such portraits, as we shall see, were revived in some Romanesque Bibles.

In a few instances in the Syriac Bible, however, we find excerpted narrative scenes, such as that of Moses and Aaron asking the Pharaoh to leave Egypt, which introduces Genesis, but which more rightfully ought to introduce Exodus, and Job on the dungheap, introducing the Book of Job.[13] We can analyze the unusual choice of the first scene for Genesis, or discuss the synoptic quality of the second, which summarizes Job's afflictions, and discover that these scenes reflect an Eastern Byzantine tradition of narrative illustration. While this is an important, though not unexpected, finding, we must also take note that this manuscript manifests a mingling of what amounts to an author-portrait tradition and a narrative tradition like that we have just seen. Whether portraiture or narration, however, the prefacing of each book in this manner leads to an evenness of treatment that yields few surprises, except for unusual iconographical choices such as the seemingly out-of-place Moses and Pharaoh miniature.

It is out of this tradition of introductory embellishment for each book of the Bible and its preface that the illumination of major English Romanesque Bibles seems to have evolved. The

---

[12] J. Leroy, *Les manuscrits syriaques à peintures conservés dans les bibliothèques de l'Europe et d'Orient* (Paris, 1964), 208 ff.; Weitzmann, *Late Antique and Early Christian Book Illumination* (New York, 1977), 17, 107–11.

[13] K. Weitzmann, *Late Antique*, 107–11.

books of the Old Testament are normally introduced by initials containing the portraits of heroes or prophets.[14] For instance, in the earliest illuminated English Bible, now divided between the Lincoln Cathedral Library (MS. A.I.2) and the Trinity College Library (MS. B.5.2) in Cambridge, portraits of Joshua and Ruth are placed within medallions in the introductory letter of their respective books.[15] But further investigation reveals that of the ninety-nine illuminated initials introducing individual books, only thirteen are figurative—the rest are foliate. Singled out for pictorial representation are Joshua receiving the Lord's command, Ruth, Joel, Jonah, Haggai, Zachariah, Ezra, Esther, Judith with the head of Holofernes, Matthew, Mark, and John, and Luke in an initial introducing the Acts of the Apostles. Thus some prophets, heroes, and evangelists receive pictorial emphasis, but surprisingly, the books of the Pentateuch, of Samuel and Kings, and of the major prophets are provided with decoration in a lower key, as one can see in table 1, where decorative letters are represented as °, figurative initials as *, and miniatures as []. The same evenness of effect is apparent in the spectacular Winchester Bible where historiated initials (*) introduce almost every book.[16]

In contrast to this treatment, we must remember, however, that the narrative tradition is equally strong in some regions during the Romanesque period, as manifested in such manuscripts as the Roda (Paris, Bibliothèque Nationale, MS. lat. 6)

---

[14] C. M. Kauffmann, *Romanesque Manuscripts 1066–1190*, ed. J. J. G. Alexander, *A Survey of Manuscripts Illuminated in the British Isles*, vol. 3 (London, 1975), and W. Cahn, *Romanesque Bible Illumination* (Ithaca, NY, 1982). See also F. Wormald, "Bible Illustration in Medieval Manuscripts," in G. W. H. Lampe, ed., *The Cambridge History of the Bible*, vol. 2, *The West from the Fathers to the Reformation* (Cambridge, 1969), 309–37.

[15] Kauffmann, *Romanesque Manuscripts*, 59–60, illus. 30–33.

[16] Kauffmann, *Romanesque Manuscripts*, 108–12, with previous bibliography. The Dover Bible (Cambridge, Corpus Christi College, MS. 3–4), also shown in the chart, reveals a similar uniformity in its preponderance of thirty-eight historiated initials compared with only 19 decorative ones: ibid., 97–98, illus. 188–91.

Table 1
Distribution of illuminations in English Romanesque Bibles

° = Decorative initials
* = Historiated initials
[] = Miniatures
() = Missing

	Lincoln	Dover	Bury	Lambeth	Winchester
Jerome prol.	°		° °	* °	*
Genesis	°		([])	[]*	*
Exodus	°	*	([])	(*)	*
Leviticus	°	°	([])	*	*
Numbers	°	*	[]	[]°	*
Deuteronomy	°	*	[]	°	(°)
Joshua	*	°	([])	(°)([])	*
Judges	°	*	([])	([])	(*)
Ruth	*	*	°	°[]*	°
1 Samuel	°	*	°[]°	°([])	[]*
2 Samuel	°	*	°	([])*	*
3 Kings	°	°	°	*([]?)°	*
4 Kings	°	*	°	([])°	*
Isaiah	°	*	([])°*	(°)[]*	*
Jeremiah	°	*	[]°	(°)([])	*
Lamentations				°	
Baruch				*	
Jeremiah's letter				*	
Ezekiel	°	°	°[]*	[]*	*
Daniel	°	°	° °	**[]**°	*
Hosea	°	*	°	°**	*
Joel	*	*		*	*
Amos	°	*	°*	°*	*
Obadiah	°	*			*
Jonah	*	*	°		
Micah	°	*	*	*	*
Habukkuk		*	° °	**°	
Nahum	°		°	°*	

Zephaniah	°	*	°	° °	*
Haggai	*	*	°	°	*
Zechariah	*	*	° °	**	*
Malachi	°	*	°	°*	*
Job	°	(°)	°[]°	°([]?)	
Psalms		*°°		****°°*°	****
Proverbs	°	*			*
Ecclesiastes	°	°			*
Canticles	°	*			*
Wisdom	°	*			*
Ecclesiasticus	°	*			*
Chronicles	°	*			*
Ezra	*	°			*
Esther	*	°			
Tobit	°	°			
Judith	*	°			[]
1 Maccabees	°	*			[]
2 Maccabees	°	°			
Matthew	*	*			
Mark	*	°			*
Luke	°	*			*
John	*	*			*
Acts	*	*			
Peter	°	*°			*
Simon	°				
John	°	°			
2, 3 John	°	**			
Apocalypse	°	*			
Pauline epistles	°	****°°			*

and Farfa or Ripoll Bibles (Rome, Biblioteca Apostolica Vaticana, MS. Vat. lat. 5729) that have extensive pen-drawn miniatures, and in the frescoes of many churches such as Saint-Savin-sur-Gartempe in France or Sant' Angelo in Formis near Capua in Italy,[17] as well as in the carved capitals of many Romanesque churches and cloisters.

Indeed the development of extensive pictorial narrative in twelfth-century English manuscripts is particularly evident in the increasing number of prefatory miniatures to Psalters, such as the St. Albans Psalter with some forty full-page Old and New Testament scenes.[18] But perhaps we should apply some caution when interpreting this growing narrative tradition in English Romanesque art, for we can also detect an unevenness of treatment in some English Bibles that suggests a strengthening didactic tradition and a shift in its thrust. Such major examples as the Bury Bible (Cambridge, Corpus Christi College, MS. 2) and the Lambeth Bible (London, Lambeth Palace and Maidstone, Museum of Art) appear to have a selective, if not focused and programmatic, series of miniatures that should not be regarded merely as stages on the way to satisfy a need for more developed narrative sequence. In spite of lacunae and conflicting descriptions of both of these manuscripts, we can find patterns of emphasis which emerge by means of concentrations of historiated initials and miniatures interspersed at only selected points among the standard fare of decorative initials.

The great Bury Bible, produced at Bury St. Edmunds about 1135 by Master Hugo, and now at Corpus Christi College (MS. 2) in Cambridge, originally contained twelve miniatures, of which only six remain, as well as three historiated initials, and thirty-nine elaborate decorated letters (table 1).[19] The first

---

[17] Extensive cycles of Romanesque frescoes can be found in Saint' Angelo in Formis near Capua, and in the nave vault of Saint-Savin-sur-Gartempe in western France. See also, P. J. Collins, "Narrative Bible Cycles in Medieval Art and Drama," in C. Davidson, C. J. Gianakaris, and J. H. Stroupe, eds., *The Drama in the Middle Ages: Comparative and Critical Essays* (New York, 1982), 25–42.

[18] For the development in England, see O. Pächt, *The Rise of Pictorial Narrative in Twelfth Century England* (Oxford, 1962) and for the St. Albans Psalter, Pächt, C. R. Dodwell, and F. Wormald, *The St. Albans Psalter* (London, 1960).

[19] Kaufmann, *Romanesque Manuscripts*, 88–90; and idem, "The Bury Bible," *Journal of the Warburg and Courtauld Institutes* 29 (1966): 60–81. The best description of the contents is to be found in M. R. James, *A*

seven books of the Old Testament would have had miniatures, but of this group, only those for Numbers, showing Aaron and Moses counting the Israelites, and for Deuteronomy, where they expound the Law to the Israelites, have survived. A miniature of Elkanah, Hannah, and Penninah and the birth of Samuel introduces the Book of Samuel, and one of Job on the dungheap confronted by his wife opens the Book of Job. Three of the major prophets, Isaiah, Jeremiah (fig. 3), and Ezekiel, were also introduced by miniatures (the one for Isaiah is now missing). In addition, three historiated initials showing Isaiah, Amos (fig. 4), and Micah begin the texts of their appropriate books, giving Isaiah, however, a double pictorial accentuation. The emphasis here therefore appears to be on the early historical books—the *ante* and *sub lege*, the linking of the Law and the prophesies through the story of the birth of Samuel, who was the last of the great judges and the first of the prophets—and on the four major prophets. This distribution of miniatures amid the prevalence of decorative initials does not appear to be merely a result of a dependence on available models; it is rather a concentration of images making this specific didactic statement through pictorial emphasis.

An even more remarkable disparity and focused message occurs in the illustration of the Lambeth Bible, believed to have been illuminated at St. Augustine's, Canterbury, circa 1140–1150.[20] Now containing nineteen decorative initials and twenty-four historiated ones, it originally singled out fourteen books in the Old Testament volume for introductory miniatures, of which only six survive: Genesis, Numbers, Joshua, Ruth, Isaiah, Jeremiah, Ezekiel, and Daniel (table 1). These do not appear to be merely erratic elaborations inserted into a book which other-

Descriptive Catalogue of the Manuscripts in the Library of Corpus Christi College Cambridge (Cambridge, 1912), 1:3–8.

[20] C. R. Dodwell, *The Great Lambeth Bible* (London, 1959); idem, *The Canterbury School of Illumination, 1066–1200*, 48 ff, 81 ff.; Kauffmann, *Romanesque Manuscripts*, 99–100; D. Denny, "Notes on the Lambeth Bible," *Gesta* 16 (1977): 51–64; R. M. Thompson, *Manuscripts from St. Albans Abbey, 1066–1235*, (Totowa, NJ, 1982), 31–33, no. 81; Cahn, *Romanesque Bibles*, 171, 180, 191, 261 no. 34.

Fig. 3. Cambridge, Corpus Christi College, MS. 2, Bury Bible, fol. 245v. Introductory Miniature to Jeremiah.

Fig. 4. Cambridge, Corpus Christi College, MS. 2, Bury Bible, fol. 324r. Initial introducing Amos.

wise has a fairly uniform array of historiated, figurative, and decorative initials. The Genesis and Numbers frontispieces are, I believe, yet another manifestation of the *ante* and *sub lege* themes mentioned above. In addition, the Genesis page contains unusual overtones of prefigurations of the redemption of man in the story of Abraham, rather than of the Fall of man itself, of the vision of the true God or the church in Jacob's dream, and of the tomb and altar of Christ's sacrifice, in the anointing of the stone of Bethel—prefigurations condensing in one miniature the unity of the Old and New Testaments by employing telling references to Christ's sacrifice.[21] The Numbers frontispiece is a two-thirds-page miniature showing Moses delivering the Law to the Israelites and the Levites carrying the ark and bringing offerings to the tabernacle.[22] A miniature occupying only one-third of a page introduces the Book of Ruth, a heroine portrait in three scenes showing Ruth gleaning, bringing the grain to Naomi, and lying at Boaz's feet, further amplified by a historiated initial at the beginning of the text showing Ruth giving barley to Boaz and Boaz's compact with his kinsmen.[23] The opening folios for Joshua, Judges, the four books of Kings, and Job are missing, each containing approximately one page of text and possibly a miniature, although such speculation as to the exact nature of the decoration that preceded these books in most cases must remain tenuous.[24]

---

[21] Dodwell, *Lambeth Bible*, 20, plate 1.

[22] Ibid., 22, plate 2.

[23] Ibid., 24, plate 3.

[24] Published information concerning these lacunae has been contradictory or ambiguous. Examination of the manuscript reveals that in each case approximately one side of a folio worth of text is missing, and stubs of excised folios are visible between fols. 133/134, 150/151, 164/165, 181/182, confirming missing folios before each book of Kings. Moreover, along the inner margin of fol. 182r at the top left, mid-point, and bottom left corner are faint imprints from roundels which would have been part of the frame around a facing miniature such as found around the Isaiah frontispiece on folio 198r. I am grateful to the librarian of Lambeth Palace for his cooperation in allowing me to examine this precious manuscript. A brief note, "Additional *Lacunae* in the Lambeth Bible," detailing the problem and the evidence, appeared in *Gesta* 28 (1989): 127–29.

Nevertheless, it is evident that the major and truly astonishing decorative emphases have been reserved for the books of
the Prophets. Even the minor prophets receive pictorial representation in historiated initials: Amos and Michah, Joel, Nahum,
Habakkuk, Hosea, Baruch, Zecharia, and Malachi (see table 1).
These initials would appear to be a continuation of the portrait-
type *incipit* found in the Syriac Bible referred to earlier and
which was revived in the Lincoln Bible.[25] For some of the
major prophets, however, the decorative openings have been
elaborated even beyond those of the Bury Bible. Isaiah is introduced by the Tree of Jesse, a pictorialization of that prophesy of
Isaiah of the genealogy of Christ, "And there shall come forth
a rod out of the stem of Jesse, and a branch shall grow out of
his roots."[26] Although this is an early representation of a
theme which was to gain considerable popularity throughout
the remainder of the Middle Ages,[27] it is here already elaborated with four prophets in the lower medallions, personifications
of Mercy and Truth, Righteousness and Peace in the middle
ones, and Ecclesia between two apostles and the Synagogue
between Abraham and Moses in the upper ones. Above the
elongated figure of the Virgin in the center is a medallion with
God and seven doves—the gifts of the Holy Spirit. This superb
diagrammatic page, rich in its didactic implications, is followed
by a historiated initial showing the martyrdom of Isaiah by
being sawn asunder.[28] A similarly accentuated opening proba-

----

[25] A tradition of illustrations introducing the books of the prophets,
usually standing "author portraits," persisted in Byzantine manuscripts
of the tenth through thirteenth centuries: see John Lowden, *Illuminated
Prophet Books: A Study of Byzantine Manuscripts of the Major and Minor
Prophets* (College Park and London, 1988).

[26] Isaiah 11.1; Dodwell, *Lambeth Bible*, 26, plate 4.

[27] See A. Watson, *The Early iconography of the Tree of Jesse* (Oxford
and London, 1934).

[28] This apocryphal martyrdom is based upon an oblique reference by
St. Paul in his Epistle to the Hebrews (2.32–37): "and the prophets who
by faith conquered kingdoms ... but others were racked, not accepting
deliverance, that they might find a better resurrection ... they were
stoned, they were cut asunder." See Kauffmann, *Romanesque Bibles*, illus.
192.

bly introduced Jeremiah, but now both an initial, possibly historiated, and a folio, possibly containing a miniature, are missing.[29] The Bury Bible has a miniature showing Jeremiah pointing to the destruction of Jerusalem (fig. 3) that reinforces the probability of a major decorative emphasis.

In any case, Ezekiel is introduced by a miniature and is followed by a historiated initial.[30] The prophet is shown blessed by the hand of God and lifted by his hair to the door of the inner gate. Below is the vision of the one man clothed in linen with the ink horn, who subsequently marks the foreheads of the righteous while his armed companions slay the unrighteous. In the initial, Ezekiel is shown eating the roll and shaving, a prefiguration of John eating the book in the Book of Revelation.[31]

But it is for the Book of Daniel that we find an extraordinarily heavy pictorial emphasis. Two prologues to this book open with historiated initials with two portraits of the prophet. The book itself is prefaced with a frontispiece showing Nebuchadnezzar's dream of the large image, the Wise Men being consulted, Daniel before Nebuchadnezzar, the three Hebrew youths praying, Daniel's vision, Nebuchadnezzar venerating Daniel, the adoration of the golden statue and the three youths in the fiery furnace (fig. 5). The text commences with a further historiated initial showing the apocryphal incident of Habakkuk, being lowered by an angel, bringing food and drink to Daniel in the

---

[29] Kauffmann, *Romanesque Manuscripts*, 99, states an initial is peeled off fol. 22v [*sic*], actually fol. 222v, where the initial could have been a column high; Dodwell, *Lambeth Bible*, 37, note 5, states a folio is missing before Jeremiah. A stub is visible between fols. 222 and 223, and Jeremiah begins at 2.5 or at a point equal to approximately a page of missing text. The other side of this missing folio, therefore, could have contained a full-page miniature.

[30] Dodwell, *Lambeth Bible*, 28, plate 5.

[31] This subject is illustrated in a copy of Haimon of Auxerre's commentary on Ezechiel and in the Roda Bible in Paris (Paris, Bibliothèque Nationale, MS. lat. 12302, fol. 1r, and MS. lat. 6, vol. 3, fol. 45r). See Neuss, *Das Buch Ezechiel in Theologie und Kunst bis zum Ende des XII. Jahrhunderts* (Münster, 1912). Both are illustrated in Kauffmann, *Romanesque Manuscripts*, figs. 30–31.

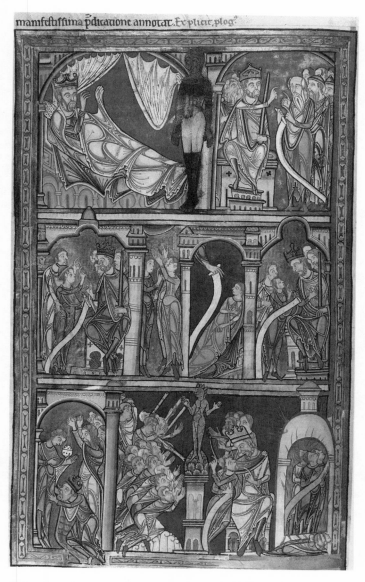

Fig. 5. London, Lambeth Palace, MS. 3, Lambeth Bible, fol. 285v. Frontispiece to Daniel.

Fig. 6. London, Lambeth Palace, MS. 3, Lambeth Bible, fol. 286. Opening Initial to Daniel with Habakkuk Lowered by Angel into Lion's Den.

lion's den (fig. 6). But this is not all, for within the text of the book, beginning verse 19 of chapter 3, "Tunc Nabuchodonosor ... " (which begins the passage in which the king becomes furious and has the Hebrew youths thrown into the furnace), the letter *T* contains the standing figure of the king; and the beginning of chapter 13, which recounts the story of Susanna and the elders, is accentuated with a decorative letter. For this book alone, in a manuscript which ordinarily has a single historiated or decorative letter commencing each book, we find one decorative and four figurative initials, as well as one extensively narrated frontispiece. Why?

It has been noted that many of the incidents depicted in the Daniel frontispiece—and indeed this is also true for the Ezekiel page mentioned previously—are very close to an even more extensive cycle of illustrations concerning these prophets in the Roda Bible in Paris (Bibliothèque Nationale MS. lat. 6), a Catalan manuscript of the mid-eleventh century. This, and the similar Ripoll Bible in Rome (Biblioteca Apostolica Vaticana, Cod. Vat. lat. 5729), appear to manifest a continuation of the lavishly illustrated type of Bible stemming from the tradition of the Ashburnham Pentateuch.[32] In the Roda Bible, the story of Daniel covers five full pages. Students of the Lambeth Bible, however, have been careful to avoid attributing these similarities to any direct contact, over perhaps a century in time, between these manuscripts, except to acknowledge that the illuminator may have had access to some other model stemming from the same tradition.[33] While I believe this view is correct, I do not feel that the particular choice of miniatures in the Lambeth or Bury Bibles depended merely on the availability of certain pictorial models, and that the exclusion of other frontispieces was due to the lack thereof. It may well be that this

---

[32] Cahn, *Romanesque Bible Illumination*, 292–93, nos. 148 and 150; W. Neuss, *Die katalanische Bibelillustration um die Wende des ersten Jahrtausends und die altspanische Buchmalerei* (Bonn and Leipzig, 1922), 10–34, from which, however, one must piece together the contents of this manuscript and the similar Ripoll Bible in Rome.

[33] See the comparisons between the Lambeth Bible and the Roda Bible in Kauffmann, *Romanesque Manuscripts*, figs. 36–39.

selection reflects a larger phenomenon with far wider implications for the entire Romanesque period.

Certainly the story of Daniel, particularly the miraculous salvation of the three youths in the fiery furnace, was a widely popular motif since Early Christian times. But in the early Romanesque period, especially in Spain, where there was almost a fanatical preoccupation with the Apocalypse, and the Beatus Commentary on the Apocalypse became a liturgical book, we find Jerome's commentary on the Book of Daniel appended to many such manuscripts.[34] Often they were illustrated, as in the miniature of the writing on the wall at Belshazzar's feast in the Morgan Beatus (MS. M. 644), or of Nebuchadnezzar and Daniel as he relates his dream of the tree and the beasts to the prophet in the Silos Apocalypse (London, British Library, MS. Add. 11695).[35] Daniel, because of his visionary, one might say apocalyptic, prophesies of destruction of the Old Order, of the Coming of Christ and of his Second Coming, and of the inevitable Last Judgment, was regarded as an Old Testament forerunner to John and his visions of the Second Coming. These Spanish representations of the Book of Daniel reflect a similar emphasis found in the Lambeth Bible. John Williams has noted that the Jerome Commentary of Daniel served a dual purpose—an Old Testament "warning about and a guarantee of victory over threats to orthodoxy from within the Christian fold" as well as against the continuing battles in Spain against the enemies of the church, the Muslims.[36] It is precisely these concerns which dominate much of later Romanesque dogma and art. As the church increasingly reacted against these threats and even took the offensive, Daniel and the other major prophets were given the role as principal spokesmen in a propagandistic campaign of continuing attacks against a variety

---

[34] W. Neuss, *Die Apokalypse des Hl. Johannes in der altspanischen und altchristlichen Bibel-Illustration* (Münster, 1931); J. Williams, "The Beatus Commentaries and Spanish Bible Illustration," in *Actas del simposio para el estudio de los códices del 'Commentario al Apocalipsis; de Beato de Liébana* (Madrid, 1980), 1:211–13, 219.

[35] John Williams, *Early Spanish Manuscript Illumination* (New York, 1977), 77, plate 19a and 126, plate 39.

[36] Williams, *Early Spanish Manuscript Illumination*, 27.

of heretical movements, and of consistent, virulent anti-Semit-ism.[37] A combination of both motifs has been carefully studied by Jean French in reference to the iconographical program of the tympanum at Beaulieu-sur-Dordogne, and Thomas Hoving has shown that the magnificent Bury St. Edmunds Cross at the Cloisters (fig. 7) is riddled with sharp rebukes of the Jews for re-jecting Christ as the Savior.[38] The arms and shaft of this cross are lined with prophets holding scrolls containing their prophesies, a sculptural reflection of the prophet portraits we have seen in the initials of English Romanesque Bibles (cf. figs. 4 and 8).

These carved busts also have a processional quality which recalls developments taking place in liturgical drama at the time.[39] It was apparently customary by the twelfth century to perform, or include in the readings for the Christmas day or the week thereafter, a liturgical play known as the *Ordo Prophetarum* (or procession of prophets) in which the preacher calls forth a succession of witnesses to make their utterances concerning the coming of Christ.[40] This play in turn was derived from a fifth- or sixth-century sermon, erroneously believed in the Middle Ages to be by St. Augustine, entitled *Sermon Against the Jews, Pagans, and Arians concerning the Creed.*[41] In England, this play

---

[37] For more on the role of heresy in Romanesque art, see Walter Cahn, "Heresy and the Interpretation of Romanesque Art," in *Essays for George Zarnecki: Romanesque and Gothic*, ed. N. Stratford (Woodbridge, Suffolk, 1986).

[38] J. French, "The Innovative Imagery of the Beaulieu Portal Pro-gram, Sources and Significance" (Ph.D. diss., Cornell University, 1972); T. Hoving, "The Bury St. Edmunds Cross," *The Metropolitan Museum of Art Bulletin* (June 1964): 317–40.

[39] An analagous reflection of liturgical drama may have occurred at Bury St. Edmunds: see Elizabeth Parker McLachlan, "Possible Evidence for Liturgical Drama at Bury St. Edmunds in the Twelfth Century," *Proceedings of the Suffolk Institute of Archeology and History* 34, no. 4 (1980): 255–61.

[40] K. Young, "Ordo Prophetarum," *Transactions of the Wisconsin Academy of Sciences, Arts and Letters* 20 (1921): 1–82; idem, *The Drama of the Medieval Church*, 2:125–71.

[41] The *Ordo Prophetarum* is taken from chapters 11 through 16 of this sermon: E. N. Stone, *A Translation of Chapters XI–XVI of the Pseudo-Au-gustinian Sermon Against Jews, Pagans and Arians, Concerning the Creed*, University of Washington Publications in Language and Literature, vol. 4, no. 3 (Seattle, 1928), 195–214.

Fig. 7. New York, The Metropolitan Museum of Art, The Cloisters Collection, 1963. (63.12), Bury St. Edmunds Cross, mid-twelfth century.

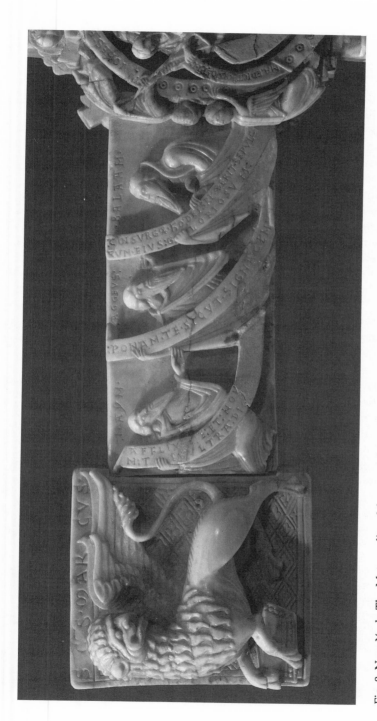

Fig. 8. New York, The Metropolitan Museum of Art, The Cloisters Collection, 1963. (63.12), Bury St. Edmunds Cross, mid-twelfth century. Detail of prophets.

was read for the second nocturn of the fourth Sunday in Advent.[42] The witnesses who give testimony are the Jews' own prophets, Isaiah, Jeremiah, Daniel, Moses, David, and Habakkuk; New Testament personages such as Simeon, Zacharias, Elizabeth, and John; and gentiles such as Virgil, Nebudchadnezzar, and the Erythraean Sibyl. The *Ordo Prophetarum* was frequently included as a third part of the *Mystère d'Adam*, a mid-twelfth-century Anglo-Norman play also performed in the Christmas season.[43]

It is perhaps no coincidence that the pronouncements of the prophets become a part of the liturgy at this season. Christ's reference to Daniel's vision, quoted in St. Matthew (24.15–35), "When you see the abomination of desolation, which was spoken of by Daniel the prophet, standing in the holy place ...," and the commentary on it by St. Jerome, as well as readings from Daniel and Ezekiel with commentaries on them, were adapted as lessons in the transitional period from the end of the liturgical year to the beginning of the next with the Advent season.[44] The End before the prophesied Beginning. Moreover, lessons from Isaiah are read throughout the first three weeks of Advent, and then, just before Christmas, the story of the three youths in the fiery furnace from Daniel is read on Ember Saturday of the third week of Advent.

Further confirmation of a heightened emphasis on the role of Daniel as a major protagonist in the liturgy and as a major spokesman against infidel and heretic alike is the appearance in the twelfth century of the *Play of Daniel*. Two versions have come down to us, one attributed to Hilarius, a student of Abelard, and a second written at the cathedral school of Beauvais, presumably both of about 1140, a date which coincides

---

[42] Ibid., 199.

[43] P. Studer, *Le Mystère d'Adam, An Anglo-Norman Drama of the Twelfth Century* (Manchester, 1918); E. N. Stone, *Adam, A Religious Play of the Twelfth Century* (Seattle, 1928); J. A. Dane, "Clerical Propaganda in the Anglo-Norman *Representacio Ade*," *Philological Quarterly* 62 (1983): 241–51.

[44] J. Taylor, "Prophetic 'Play' and Symbolist 'Plot' in the Beauvais *Daniel*," in C. Davidson, C. J. Gianakaris, and J. H. Stroupe, eds., *The Drama in the Middle Ages: Comparative and Critical Essays* (New York, 1982), 25–42.

with the presumed dates of the creation of the Bury Cross and Lambeth Bible.[45] The emphasis in this Old Testament play is on Belshazzar's feast and Daniel's interpretation of the writing on the wall, and the story of Daniel being cast into the lion's den, his miraculous (and apocryphal) feeding by Habakkuk, concluding with his release from prison by Darius and Daniel's prophesy of the coming of Christ. Jerome Taylor has discussed this play in relation to the liturgy of Advent and makes the provocative suggestion that it might have been intended to be performed after matins and before the Midnight Mass of Christmas.[46] Karl Young observed that it was also connected with the *Ordo Prophetarum* and the Pseudo-Augustinian sermon against the Jews since Daniel's prophesy at the end of the play, *"Cum venerit Sanctus Sanctorum, cessabit unctio*: When the Most Holy One shall have come, your anointing shall cease," is derived, not from the Vulgate text, but from the sermon, and is repeated in the *Ordo*.[47] That this play became associated with the liturgy of the Christmas season at this time, and that it is another reflection of the twelfth-century preoccupation with eschatalogical visions, makes the emphasis on prophets in Romanesque art all the more understandable. Émile Mâle stressed the impact of liturgical drama on medieval art, particularly on the sculpture of church façades; and although this influence is downplayed in modern scholarship, there can be no doubt that in some instances, such as the façade of Notre-Dame-la-Grande at Poitiers where four prophets lead us from the Fall at the far left to the Annunciation at the right of the arch, and in the selection of prophets on the door jambs of churches at Verona, Cremona, and Ferrara, there are explicit references to the Pseudo-Augustinian sermon and the *Ordo Prophetarum*.[48] I cannot insist on a direct parallel with the

---

[45] See Young, *Drama of the Medieval Church*, 2:276–306; W. L. Smolden, trans. and ed., *The Play of Daniel: A Medieval Liturgical Drama* (London, 1960); and J. Taylor, "Prophetic 'Play' and Symbolist Plot." The only surviving copy is a manuscript in the British Library, MS. Egerton 2615, probably of 1227–1234, but it is generally agreed that the play originates from circa 1140: ibid., 40, note 1.

[46] Taylor, "Prophetic 'Play,' " 33.

[47] Young, *Drama of the Medieval Church*, 2:304–6.

[48] É. Mâle, *Religious Art in France. The Twelfth Century: A Study of the*

Lambeth Bible, for the actual choice of scenes in the miniature differs from the events of these liturgical dramas. Nevertheless, the weight of the admittedly circumstantial evidence in the contemporary references to Daniel in the liturgy, para-liturgical drama, in the sculpture of some Romanesque façades, and, we should now add, in the selective decoration of some Romanesque Bibles suggests that these are all reflections of a larger context. One can say that the Romanesque period is a period of prophets, a period of ecstatic, apocalyptic images on church portals (as at Moissac), a period of church militancy, exemplified by the crusades against the Muslims in the Holy Land, a period of conflict against a wave of new heresies that made the Pseudo-Augustinian sermon an appropriate revival. Seen in this light, the proclamatory emphasis on lesser prophets with their scrolls, on the eschatalogical visions of the major prophets, on the Judaic genealogy of Christ and on the Judaic heroes and heroines who prefigured the triumph of the Christian era seems entirely consistent with the prevalent attitudes and struggles of the church during the twelfth century. These concerns are particularly reflected in the multitude of prophet initials and visionary miniatures of the Bury and Lambeth Bibles, and encapsulated in the opening initials to Habakkuk in the latter where the prophet appears above the crucifix between the defeated Synagogue and the triumphant Ecclesia.[49] Perhaps we cannot speak of a specific, focused program in the Bury and Lambeth Bibles, but I believe that we can see that the selection of the images in them is not so much the result a scant supply of available models to copy, many of which are not really traceable to earlier sources, as they are of a deliberate choice to articulate those books of the Bible that carried the message most appropriate for the concerns of the day.

Origins of Medieval Iconography, ed. H. Bober, M. Mathews, trans. (Princeton, 1978), 143–53, especially 145–48 and figs. 129 and 130.

[49] Cahn, *Romanesque Bibles*, 170, fig. 132.

Biblical Stories in Windows: Were They Bibles for the Poor?

Madeline H. Caviness

A mong functions claimed for monumental picture cycles in the Middle Ages is that of teaching the Scriptures, a claim which raises a number of troubling questions and quibbles: if so, was it really "Scripture"—the Vulgate Bible—that was taught, or selected stories in some apocryphal or even vernacular version? What about exegesis—without any commentary were not some biblical events incomprehensible in Christian terms? And can pictures be "read" in any way that is comparable to the reading of a book? These are questions I will address in examining the treatment of biblical subjects in stained glass of the twelfth and thirteenth centuries.

It is worth remarking at the outset that these windows were created well before the manuscript recension that has come to be known as the *Biblia pauperum* or Bible of the poor was invented.[1] Yet the formula that the treatment of biblical subjects in monumental art somehow provided "Bibles for the Poor" was commonplace in writings about stained glass earlier in this century. To quote, for instance, from le Couteur's popular book, published by the Society for the Promotion of Christian Knowledge in 1926:

---

[1] For the beginnings of that manuscript tradition, shortly before 1300, and its later title see: Gerhard Schmidt, *Die Armenbibeln des XIV Jahrhunderts* (Graz, 1959), 41, 49; Avril Henry, *Biblia Pauperum: Facsimile and Edition* (Ithaca, 1987), 1–38.

many people received the greater part of their religious instruction from the miracle plays or from the windows and walls of their parish churches. Hence the coloured windows served two distinct purposes, decoration and education. They formed, in fact, together with the almost equally common mural paintings, the picture-books of the Middle Ages, by which the clergy taught their congregations, fully realising that "that which the illiterate cannot comprehend from writing could be made plain to them by the pictures."[2]

This was still the justification for this art form that I most frequently heard when I was working on sills and scaffolds in Canterbury Cathedral two decades ago, and it struck me as an essentially modern, protestant, and socialist way to vindicate much medieval art.

Some support for this interpretation, however, is apparently to be found among medieval writers, as suggested by le Couteur's use of quotation marks for his final phrase. Early in the fifth century Paulinus of Nola justified the extensive biblical cycle that he had painted on the walls of his basilica because it drew in

> peasant people, not devoid of religion, but not able to read ... [who] look wonderingly around, their rude minds piously beguiled.... Therefore it seemed to us useful work gaily to embellish [St.] Felix' houses all over with sacred paintings in order to see whether the spirit of the peasants would not be surprised by this spectacle and undergo the influence of the coloured sketches which are explained by inscriptions over them, so that the script may make clear what the hand has exhibited. Maybe that, when they all in turn show and reread to each other what has been painted, their thoughts will turn more slowly to eating.... When one reads the saintly histories of chaste works, virtue induced by pious example steals upon one; he who thirsts

---

[2] John Dolberl le Couteur, *English Mediaeval Painted Glass* (London, 1926), 39.

is quenched with sobriety, the result being a forgetting of the desire for too much wine.[3]

The famous letter of St. Gregory the Great to Bishop Serenus of Marseille (ca. 600 AD) chides him for allowing the destruction of images, and offers a similar justification of them: "to adore images is one thing; to teach with their help what should be adored is another. What Scripture is to the educated, images are to the ignorant, who see through them what they must accept; they read in them what they cannot read in books.... It is not without reason that tradition permits the deeds of the saints to be depicted in holy places."[4] In late twelfth-century England the anonymous author, perhaps Cistercian, of the *Pictor in carmine* referred to a "class of pictures which, as being books of the laity, can suggest divine things to the unlearned, and stir up the learned to the love of scripture."[5]

Yet these texts already suggest one modification to my title— the audience is to be defined by illiteracy, not by poverty; in the early period some are pagans, and all must be laics—or perhaps young novices—since the adult clergy could read. Furthermore, the mood is one of justification; certain effects on the populace are hoped for, though not actually observed, and these are to operate more through the emotions than through reason. Other medieval texts could be cited that express the same general idea—a very dramatic example is the famous colophon by Maius in one of the earliest Spanish Apocalypses: "I have also painted the miraculous events and the stories in a series so that

---

[3] Caecilia Davis-Weyer, *Early Medieval Art 300–1150*, Sources and Documents (Toronto, 1986), 19; the editor, however, notices that Paulinus is interested in supplying allegorical readings, presumably beyond the understanding of his clientele, and finds his "excuse somewhat disingenuous" (18).

[4] Davis-Weyer, 48.

[5] M. R. James, "Pictor in Carmine," *Archaeologia* 94 (1951): 141. This and other such texts are discussed in greater depth by Michael Camille, "Seeing and Reading: Some Visual Interpretations of Medieval Literacy and Illiteracy," *Art History* 8 (1985): 26–49. For an overview of earlier justifications for pictorial cycles, see Herbert Kessler, "Pictures as Scripture in Fifth-Century Churches," *Studia Artium Orientalis et Occidentalis* 2, fascicule 1 (1985): 17–31.

those who know them will be terrified by the future judgement and the passing of the world"; it would be hard to find a clearer statement of the affective purpose of the illustrations.[6] Yet this is in an illustrated book, and since full cycles of Apocalypse pictures are almost unheard of in the monumental media of fresco and glass painting, it carries me rather far from my topic.

The models that I have chosen for analysis, on the other hand—stained glass windows of the second half of the twelfth through the mid-thirteenth century—were a monumental art form often accessible to the public, and their sheer size, luminosity, and color intensity would guarantee their impact. The area is a rich one to investigate, since the field of glass studies is now well enough established to survey original examples, allowing one to talk broadly about the selection of subjects, the position in the buildings of different kinds of images, and to look in some detail at narrative sequences which correspond to biblical stories.[7] Whereas some windows in monastic choirs may have been intended more for the monks than the laity, and the historiated windows of the Sainte Chapelle, Louis IX's palace chapel, would have been seen principally by members of his household, most windows in the Gothic cathedrals were seen by large numbers of people who were admitted regardless of their educational level or position in society. Many of these windows were created under the patronage of lay artisan groups, the nascent merchant guilds, and I will discuss some of the selections they made.

The first questions I posed concerned the extent to which biblical subject matter was used in windows of the period, and

---

[6] New York, Morgan Library, MS. 644, fol. 293: "Inter eius decus verba mirifica storiarumque depinxi per seriem ut scientibus terreant futuri adventui peracturi saeculi." Quoted by Wilhelm Neuss, *Die Katalonischen Bibelillustration* (Bonn and Leipzig), 1922, 64 and n. 60.

[7] The study of glass has made great advances in the past thirty years through the publication of the *Corpus Vitrearum* volumes under the aegis of the Union Académique Internationale and the Comité International de l'Histoire de l'Art, though for the Cathedrals of Bourges, Chartres, and Rouen the older monographs referred to below have not yet been superceded.

whether it held any positions that might be described as normative within total glazing schemes. Thus at the outset of my
survey I took note of four kinds of biblical windows, and
marked these with a graphic code on a number of building
plans to see what could be learned about "programs" and
favorite subjects: In the accompanying figures sequences of Old
Testament events are shown by "O," as for instance in the Life
of Moses Window at Saint-Denis (fig. 1); typological windows,
(T), present the New Testament story, each event juxtaposed
with types generally lifted out of narrative sequence from the
Old Testament, but including also the Tree of Jesse as the
fulfillment of Isaiah's prophesy by the coming of Christ; symbolic subjects (S) include material from non-biblical as well as

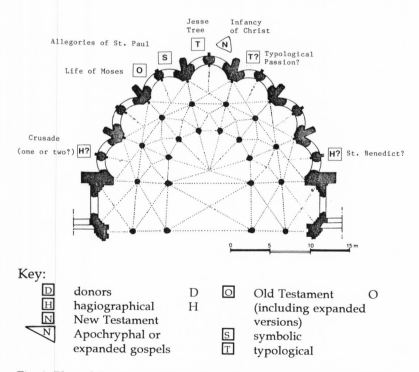

Key:

D	donors	D	O	Old Testament O
H	hagiographical	H		(including expanded
N	New Testament			versions)
N	Apochryphal or		S	symbolic
	expanded gospels		T	typological

Fig. 1. Plan of the chevet of the Abbey Church of Saint-Denis (adapted
from Louis Grodecki, *Vitraux de Saint-Denis*), with types of subjects in
the windows. Key to figs. 1–9.

biblical sources, and treat it in non-narrative ways, an example being Suger's Anagogical Window in Saint-Denis.[8] New Testament events (N) constitute gospel stories and related histories, such as the lives of apostles—differentiated if they are apocryphal, or if they are expanded beyond the biblical text; in fact this last group might have been classified as hagiographical (H) but I reserved that label for post-New Testament saints—such as Charlemagne and Benedict at Saint-Denis (the life of the latter was probably in the crypt).[9]

None of the windows known to have been in the choir of Suger's Abbey Church at Saint-Denis, consecrated in 1144, were purely narrative, and none depended directly on the Vulgate; the Infancy of Christ Window, given a place of honor with the Jesse Tree in the axial chapel, "at the head of the church" as Suger said, illustrates episodes in Pseudo-Matthew.[10] The Moses Window has inscriptions and some pictorial symbols that give each event a typological significance, even though they are represented in normal chronological order—as though one were reading a theological commentary on Exodus rather than the

---

[8] Louis Grodecki, *Les Vitraux de Saint-Denis: Etude sur le vitrail au XIIe siècle*, Corpus Vitrearum Medii Aevi, France: Etudes I (Paris, 1976), 93–94, 98–102, pl. 5, figs. 122–34.

[9] For the Crusading Window, which included Charlemagne, see most recently Elizabeth A. R. Brown and Michael W. Cothren, "The Twelfth-Century Crusading Window of the Abbey of Saint-Denis: 'Praeteritorum enim Recordatio Futurorum est Exhibitio,'" *Journal of the Warburg and Courtauld Institutes* 49 (1986): 1–40. The Benedict Window was reconstructed by Grodecki, *Vitraux de Saint-Denis*, 108–14, figs. 145–73; another panel, with St. Benedict in the cave, has been identified at Raby Castle: David O'Connor and Peter Gibson, "The Chapel Windows at Raby Castle, County Durham," *The Journal of Stained Glass* (formerly of *The British Society of Master Glass Painters*) 18 (1986–87): 127–28, pls. 5d, 6c.

[10] Erwin Panofsky, *Abbot Suger on the Abbey Church of St.-Denis and its Art Treasures*, 2d ed. (Princeton, 1979), 72–73: in his *De Administratione* Suger referred to the *Stirps Iesse in capite ecclesiae* but not to the adjacent Infancy Window even though he appears at the feet of the Virgin annunciate in it. For the iconography of this window see Michael W. Cothren, "The Infancy of Christ Window from the Abbey of Saint-Denis: A Reconsideration of Its Design and Iconography," *Art Bulletin* 68 (1986): 403–4, 413–16.

vulgate text.[11] The sequence of subjects in the windows is generally too esoteric to have been effective in teaching an ignorant laity; Hoffmann is surely right in seeing the program rather as an object of contemplation for the monks.[12]

The organization of subjects, and their defined character, is much clearer in the Benedictine choir of Canterbury Cathedral, glazed between thirty and fifty years later (fig. 2). Twelve typological widows in the choir, when complete, traced New Testament history from the Annunciation to the Passion, and the sequel to Pentecost is in the east window, next to a Jesse Tree.[13] No purely narrative New or Old Testament windows survive, and there is scarcely room for any. The lives of the saints—canonized churchmen from Stephen and Gregory to Thomas Becket—occupy (or once occupied) the tribune level of the choir, the chapels that open off the transepts, and the ambulatory of the Trinity Chapel which gave access to Becket's shrine.[14] Here, as much as at Saint-Denis, the typological windows are esoteric and private, heavily inscribed with learned verses that explain or provide a commentary on the scenes; both pictures and inscriptions were surely for reading and meditation by monks. Viewing their educational role in that context, the larger one of a "Bible of the Poor" becomes less likely, regardless that the windows fell under the gaze of countless pilgrims as they made their way to the shrine. It is in the Miracles of Thomas Becket, dramatic scenes of healing that surround the site of the shrine, that straightforward narrative takes over, of the kind that could be "read" by the illiterate; the events depicted correspond to those in contemporary prose

---

[11] Grodecki, *Vitraux de Saint-Denis*, 93–98, pls. 1, 9, 10, figs. 105–21.

[12] Konrad Hoffmann, "Sugers 'Anagogisches Fenster' in Saint-Denis," *Wallraf-Richartz-Jahrbuch* 30 (1968): 57–88.

[13] Madeline H. Caviness, *The Early Stained Glass of Canterbury Cathedral ca. 1175–1220* (Princeton, 1977), 115–38, appendix, figs. 9–20, figs. 19–63; M. H. Caviness, *The Windows of Christ Church Cathedral Canterbury*, Corpus Vitrearum Medii Aevi, Great Britain II (London, 1981), 79–174, pls. 60–108.

[14] Caviness, *Early Glass*, 139–50, figs. 109–20, 159–210; Caviness, *Windows of Canterbury*, 67–71, 127–28, 137–39, 158–60, 175–214, pls. 44–55, 96, 109–60.

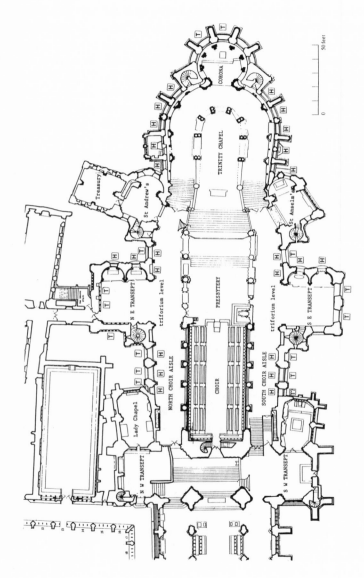

Fig. 2. Plan of the choir and east end of Christ Church Cathedral, Canterbury (adapted from Caviness, *Early Glass*), with types of subjects in the windows.

accounts, though the sequence of stories is different. The effect of these windows must have been to excite an impressionable crowd to hope for and believe in further miracles. Yet it might be mistaken to conclude that this effect was entirely devised by the clergy, since there is a strong possibility that the subjects were chosen, and the glass paid for, by lay patrons.[15]

A somewhat analogous program was devised considerably later for another monastic building which was the principal center for the cult of a recently deceased local saint, namely, the Franciscan Church of Assisi (fig. 3).[16] The upper church, which follows the reverse orientation of St. Peter's in Rome because of the slope of the site, has glass of the late thirteenth through the early fourteenth century. The position of three typological windows in the apse (at the west end) corresponds to familiar monastic use; in these, events from the birth of the Virgin to Pentecost are paired with Old Testament types. In the transept, the Creation and story of Adam and Eve on the south face the appearances of the risen Christ on the north. Single figures of apostles and saints, and four hagiographical legends, fill the nave windows, the area most accessible to pilgrims. These are supplemented by wall paintings with Old Testament subjects in the upper zone, and the famous Life of St. Francis below the windows; the frescoes and stained glass complement each other, and it is unfortunate that art historians have tended to treat them separately.[17]

The next group of plans are of thirteenth-century French Cathedrals. One of the most coherent programs is that of the Cathedral of Bourges, soon after 1200 (fig. 4). Compared with the monastic examples reviewed above, greater importance is

---

[15] Caviness, *Early Glass*, 32–33, 106.

[16] Giuseppe Marchini, *Le Vetrate dell'Umbria*, Corpus Vitrearum Medii Aevi, Italia I (Rome, 1973), 20–88, pls. 1–68.

[17] Among many monographs on the frescoes are Alastair Smart, *The Assisi Problem and the Art of Giotto: A Study of the Legend of St. Francis in the Upper Church of San Francesco, Assisi* (Oxford, 1971); on the other hand, Hans Belting, *Die Oberkirche von San Francesco in Assisi: ihre Dekoration als Aufgabe und die Genese einer neuen Wandmelerei* (Berlin, 1977), takes some of the glass into account.

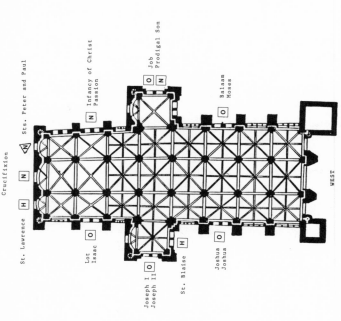

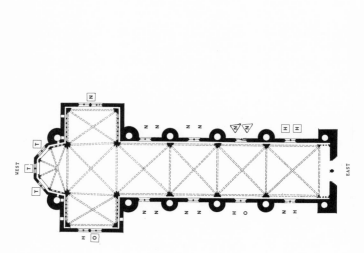

Fig. 3. Plan of the Upper Church of San Francesco in Assisi (adapted from Marchini, *Vetrate*), with types of subjects in the windows.

Fig. 5. Plan of the Cathedral of Saint-Pierre of Poitiers (adapted from Grodecki, *Journal of the Warburg and Courtauld Institutes* [1948]), with types of subjects in the windows.

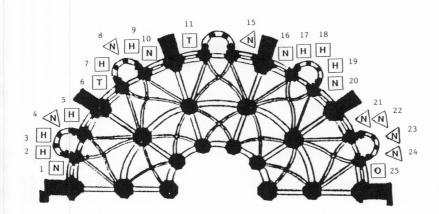

Subjects of Windows

1: Good and Bad Rich Men
2: Life of St. Mary of Egypt
3: Life of St. Nicholas
4: Life of St. Mary Magdalen
5: Relics of St. Stephen
6: Good Samaritan
7: Life of St. Denis
8: Life of Sts. Peter and Paul
9: Life of St. Martin
10: Prodigal Son
11: New Alliance

15: Last Judgement
16: Passion
17: Life of St. Lawrence
18: Stoning of St. Stephen
19: Life of St. Vincent
20: Apocalypse
21: Life of St. Thomas
22: Life of St. James the Great
23: Life of St. John Baptist
24: Life of St. John Evangelist
25: Story of Joseph

Fig. 4. Plan of the ambulatory of the Cathedral of Saint-Etienne, Bourges (adapted from Grodecki, *Journal of the Warburg and Courtauld Institutes* [1948]), with types of subjects in the windows.

given to isolated New Testament stories, but there is no sequence of windows presenting the whole gospel narrative even
in the ambulatory. Three windows contain parables, one of
them with Old Testament types (the Good Samaritan with the
fall and redemption of man), the other two unembellished (the
Good and Bad Rich Men and the Prodigal Son). There is both a
Passion Window and typological Passion or "New Alliance"
Window.[18] The New Testament subjects are supplemented by
a Last Judgement and an Apocalypse, and the parables are also
eschatalogical. A single Old Testament story stands out on the
south side—that of Joseph.[19] The chapels are given to saints'
lives, whether of the biblical or later period.

The Cathedral of Poitiers has windows of the 1160s–1170s in
the east end of the choir, and of the early thirteenth century
through the rest of the choir, transepts, and nave (fig. 5).[20]
Typological or symbolic windows are absent here, and such
extensive use of Old Testament stories is extremely rare. Despite
their predominance on the north side—a position Mâle claimed
as normative—the distribution is not regular, since they intrude
also on the south. The stories of "heroes" are singled out—Lot,
Isaac, Joseph, and Joshua with two windows each, Moses,
Balaam, and Job. Christ, and the Prodigal Son seem to find a
place among them, rather than outshining them.

What remains *in situ* of the early thirteenth-century glass of
Rouen Cathedral seems to indicate a similar distribution—two
Joseph windows (on the north) facing the Passion and the Good

---

[18] The most detailed account of these windows is still that of Charles
Cahier and Arthur Martin, *Monographie de la cathédrale de Bourges* I:
Vitraux du 13ᵉ siècle (Paris, 1841–44), 1–132, 232–41, pls. 1, 4, 5, 6, 9. A
useful summary, with recent bibliography, is in Louis Grodecki et al.,
Les Vitraux du Centre et des Pays de la Loire, Corpus Vitrearum, France:
Recensement des vitraux anciens de la France II (Paris, 1981), 168–75,
figs. 140–48.

[19] Cahier and Martin, *Bourges*, 242–44, pl. 10.

[20] The best overall description to date is still that of Louis Grodecki,
"Les vitraux de la cathédrale de Poitiers," *Congrès archéologique de France
1951* 109 (1952): 138–63. Virginia Raguin is preparing a thorough
analysis of the windows, and I am grateful to her for the loan of her
notes and slides.

Samaritan (fig. 6).[21] A fuller program, spanning the middle of the century, is preserved in the Cathedral of Auxerre (fig. 7).[22] Breakages in many windows have been filled in by subjects from elsewhere, but undisturbed panels are marked in the plan. They show a propensity for Old Testament narratives on the north side of the choir, interspersed with hagiographical windows, and a preference for New Testament events and other saints' lives on the south, including one parable. A single typological Jesse Tree is in the east wall, probably originally paired with a Life of the Virgin, now lost. Clerestory windows, as is normal in this period, for instance at Canterbury and Bourges, are filled by large figures, here prophets regularly paired with apostles.

A somewhat similar distribution is offered in the earlier glazing of the nave of Chartres Cathedral; in the west end, glass of about 1150 includes a Tree of Jesse, with an apocryphal Infancy of Christ Window, and the Passion (fig. 9).[23] The nave aisles present several hagiographical subjects, with a preference for New Testament saints on the south, which also provides an emplacement for the parable of the good Samaritan. On the north, the hagiographical windows are interspersed with two Old Testament stories, those of Noah and Joseph, and a typological Redemption Window. Chapels in the chevet concentrate hagiographical subjects together; only one window, the Apostles' Lives in the axial position, is based on the Vulgate. Chartres is unusual among Gothic monuments in employing narrative panels in some clerestory widows, as though a love of storytelling overflows, yet such sequences are kept to three or

---

[21] The only complete presentation of the glass is that of Georges Ritter, *Les vitraux de la cathédrale de Rouen: XIII, XIV, et XVI siecles, reproductions en heliotype publiees avec une introduction historique et des notices iconographiques* (Cognac Charente, 1926), 43–45, pls. 12–17.

[22] Virginia Chieffo Raguin, *Stained Glass in Burgundy during the Thirteenth Century* (Princeton, 1982), 29–39, 127–71, figs. 8–91.

[23] The most complete analysis and reproduction to date is still that of Yves Delaporte and Etienne Houvet, *Les vitraux de la cathédrale de Chartres*, 4 vols. (Chartres, 1926). Some supplementary information and recent bibliography are reported in Grodecki, *Vitraux du Centre*, 25–44.

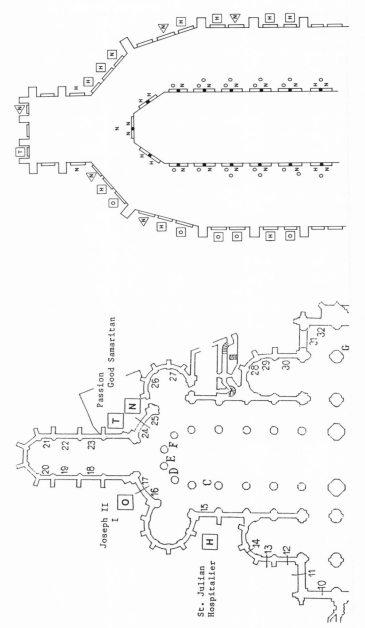

Fig. 6. Plan of the chevet of the Cathedral of Rouen (adapted from Ritter, *Les Vitraux*), with types of subjects in the windows.

Fig. 7. Plan of the Cathedral of Saint-Etienne of Auxerre (adapted from Raguin, *Burgundy*), with types of subjects in the windows.

four scenes in order to maintain a legible scale; the nave has a more regular sequence of single figures, though even some of these are also represented in a single scene, as though to provide a pictorial label for them in addition to an inscription.

Chartres also offers an unusually complete picture of the kinds of donors responsible for the glazing, since many windows contain a pictorial signature, such as a representation of them engaged in their communal activity, their arms, or an inscribed "portrait"; its incoherent program may be imputed to such individual selections (fig. 10).[24] The distribution of these votive portraits is interesting: lay corporations, their gifts represented by a "C" on the plan, dominated the lower-story glazing, apparently being first to commission windows as the bays were ready to glaze; this is also true of the nave and hemicycle clerestories. The later campaigns, in the clerestory of the straight bays of the choir and of the transepts, were dominated by wealthy individuals, both laity ("L") and ecclesiastics ("E"). In the north aisle of the nave, in sequence beginning from the west, the barrel makers presented the Noah Window—an understandable choice in view of his invention of viniculture; the tavern keepers were associated with the St. Lubin Window, emphasizing their own activities in the context of this Chartrain bishop's role as cellerer and celebrant;[25] the St. Eustace Win-

---

[24] Information on these signatures is derived from Delaporte and Houvet, *Vitraux de Chartres*. The "program" is also discussed in Caviness, *Early Glass*, 40–41, 101–2, though the dependence on Latin texts should be questioned. Wolfgang Kemp informs me that a student in his seminar at Marburg has found a single vernacular text that accords with the Charlemagne Window, whereas dependence on several Latin versions had been posited by Clark Maines, "The Charlemagne Window at Chartres Cathedral: New Considerations on Text and Image," *Speculum* 52 (1977): 801–23. I am not in agreement with Jean-Paul Deremble and Colette Manhes, *Les vitraux légendaires de Chartres: récits en images* (Paris, 1988), 16, that the appearance of some theological attitudes consistent with the early thirteenth-century date of the windows constitutes a pre-determined program. Jane Williams, "The Windows of the Trades at Chartres Cathedral" (Ph.D. diss., University of California at Los Angeles, 1987), has contested the traditional view that the "signatures" connote donors on socio-economic grounds; I am grateful to her for a frank discussion of this paper.

[25] The relation between the tavern keepers and the imagery in the St.

dow was a gift of the drapers and furriers, as if to associate their chosen saint with an aristocratic client; the Joseph Window was given by the money changers, recalling the coin for which he was sold; the St. Nicholas Window was a gift of the apothecaries; the typological Redemption Window is due to the blacksmiths, perhaps in reference to the nails of the Crucifixion. The distinctions I have made between Old and New Testaments, between Vulgate and apocryphal texts, between hagiographical and biblical subjects, were probably of little importance to these donors; each protagonist sanctifies their worldly tasks, becoming their special hero or patron.

The last glazing plan to be examined here is that of a building type that is very rare in the Gothic period, the palace chapel, represented by the Sainte Chapelle of Paris (fig. 8).[26] It was constructed and decorated by Louis IX circa 1241–1248, not only to serve the royal household but also to house the crown of thorns of Christ. The Infancy and Passion, with a Tree of Jesse, occupy traditional honored positions in the east, as at Saint-Denis and Canterbury. New Testament saints' lives flanking these fill out this era of history, and in addition a full window on the south side is given to the history of the relics of the passion (window A). By far the greatest amount of glass however, comprising about 800 subjects, is devoted to Old Testament books, beginning with Genesis on the north side (O) and continuing with Exodus, Leviticus, Numbers, Deuteronomy (with Ruth and Joshua), and Judges. The Book of Kings resumes on the south side (B), in such a way that the actions of Old Testament kings seem connected to the royal patrons who discovered the relics. Elsewhere successive coronations lead to Christ crowned with thorns in the axial window.[27] Old Testa-

---

Lubin Window has been investigated by Carole DeCosse, "The St. Lubin Window of Chartres Cathedral" (Masters thesis, Tufts University, 1984).

[26] The program is fully described and illustrated by Louis Grodecki in Marcel Aubert et al., *Les Vitraux de Notre-Dame et de la Sainte Chapelle de Paris*, Corpus Vitrearum Medii Aevi, France I (Paris, 1959), 78–84, 94–332, pls. 14–94.

[27] Aubert, *Sainte-Chapelle*, pls. 25 (M-166) and 28 (160–67), cf. pl. 52 (H-81).

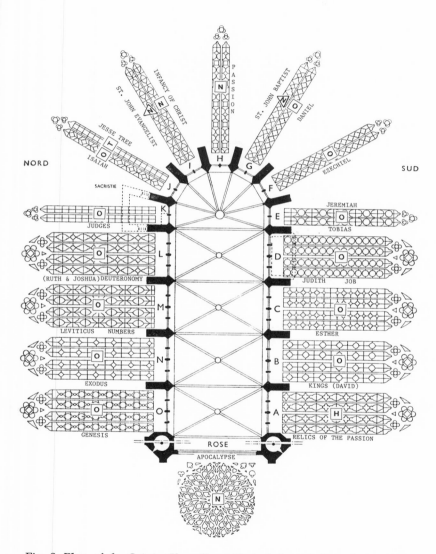

Fig. 8. Plan of the Sainte Chapelle of Paris (adapted from Aubert, *Les Vitraux de Paris*), with types of subjects in the windows.

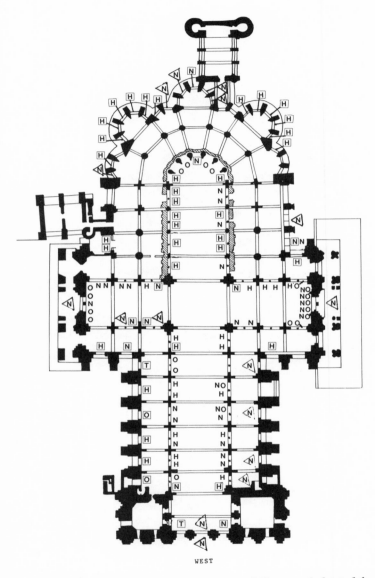

WEST

Fig. 9. Plan of the Cathedral of Notre-Dame of Chartres (adapted from Deremble and Manhes, *Les Vitraux légendaires de Chartres*), with types of subjects in the windows.

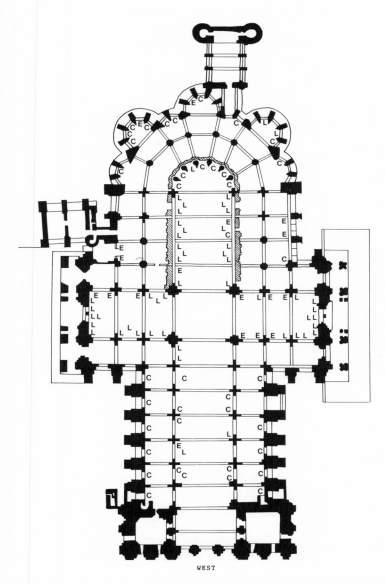

WEST

Fig. 10. Plan of the Cathedral of Notre-Dame of Chartres (adapted from Deremble and Manhes, *Les Vitraux légendaires de Chartres*), with categories of donors of the windows.

ment heroes and heroines fill out the series, including Esther, Judith and Job, and Tobias, as well as the books of Ezechiel, Daniel, and Isaiah. Sacred history is completed in the west rose by the Apocalypse, a fifteenth-century ensemble that most probably replaces an original of the same subject. Overall this is the most "bookish" program we have seen since Canterbury, no doubt carefully directed by a spiritual advisor to the king in much the same vein that had produced the *Bible moralisée* manuscripts slightly earlier. It differs from both those works, however, in that typological relationships are given far less emphasis, and there are no verbal explanations other than a few name-labels; the treatment of the Bible is relatively complete and largely historical, though it also provided moral instruction for a crusading king. Yet the windows could not be claimed as a "Bible for the Poor" since access to them was evidently restricted; and if they were used as scriptural instruction for members of the household, a theologian would have been on hand to help in their "reading."

In order to address the question of how windows with biblical events might have been "read" by the illiterate in the Middle Ages, it will be well to return to examples in the nave of Chartres, where the extent of lay patronage at least is well established.[28] Given the scale of these windows, and an organization of the narrative that is seldom like an illuminated book page, it is surely naive to think of them as book substitutes. A typical manuscript page, such as those comprising a prefatory cycle to the Great Canterbury Psalter in Paris, of about 1180, presents the story in regular registers which are comparable to lines of text in that they are to be read from the top and from the left (fig. 11). On the other hand a window that might appear superficially similar, such as the earlier central west window of Chartres which also deals with the Infancy of Christ, actually reads from the bottom up, and the sequence at times weaves

---

[28] For very useful reflection on the way in which illiterate peoples "read" pictures, based on anthropological findings, see Michael Camille, "Some Visual Implications of Medieval Literacy and Illiteracy," *Art History* 8, 1 (1985): 26–49.

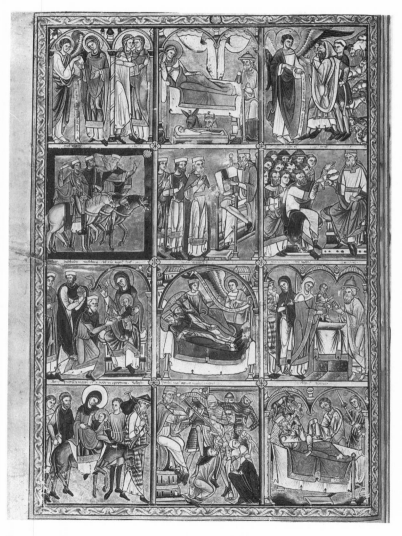

Fig. 11. Infancy cycle, the Great Canterbury Psalter in Paris, Bibliothèque Nationale, MS. lat. 8846 fol. 4v. (photo: B.N.).

from right to left and left to right in boustrophedon order, or loops up vertically to tumble the scenes.[29] By 1200 it was more frequent to use a star composition which encouraged non-linear readings, as in the typological Redemption Window of Chartres; this places emphasis on the central scenes, through their dominant position, size, and sometimes also color (fig. 12).[30] Such star formations are sometimes alternated with smaller compositional units, in a point-counterpoint system (fig. 16). To try to read such windows with the Vulgate in one hand in an attempt to control the identification and sequence of scenes can be extremely frustrating.[31] The essential point is that narrative art demands a "recitation" rather than a reading, and where verbal clues are lacking it is natural to confabulate in order to give a story that will satisfactorily explain the relationships between events and between protagonists. In this century we are familiar with this technique: we have seen picture books in language instruction intended to evoke stories directly in the new language, rather than translations. All of us in fact deal with real events and real people in this way.

---

[29] Delaporte and Houvet, *Vitraux de Chartres*, 149–55, fig. 7. Boustrophedon order has also been observed in the adjacent Passion Window: Florens Deuchler, "Le sens de la lecture: A propos du boustrophédon," *Etudes d'Art médiéval offertes à Louis Grodecki*, ed. Sumner Crosby et al. (Paris, 1981), 252–53, schéma II. Such readings of picture cycles were discussed in a pioneering article by Meyer Schapiro, "On Some Problems in the Semiotics of Visual Art: Field and Vehicle in Image-Signs," *Semiotica* 1 (1969): 223–42, esp. 231.

[30] In the St. Lubin Window red grounds are used in the center, blue in the periphery. Some of these principles of centrality have been independently noted by Wolfgang Kemp in his recent book *Sermo Corporeus: Die Erzählung der mittelalterlichen Glasfenster* (Munich, 1987). I was glad to discuss these ideas with him, but did not read his work closely before this paper went to press.

[31] The Column of Trajan presents a similar problem, its 155 scenes spiralling upward so that the spectator could scarcely be expected to keep his place in the "reading" as he walked around below; a more satisfactory way to read is one that depends on the vertical positioning of like figures, such as an aggressive, upward moving Trajan, and a Dacian unable to stand his ground, as suggested by Richard Brilliant, *Visual Narratives: Storytelling in Etruscan and Roman Art* (Ithaca, 1984), 90–108.

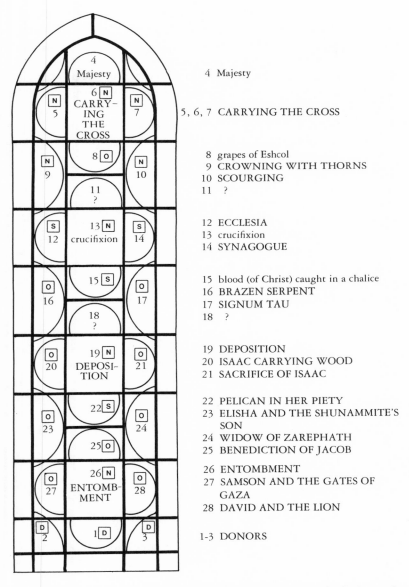

4 Majesty

5, 6, 7 CARRYING THE CROSS

8 grapes of Eshcol
9 CROWNING WITH THORNS
10 SCOURGING
11 ?

12 ECCLESIA
13 crucifixion
14 SYNAGOGUE

15 blood (of Christ) caught in a chalice
16 BRAZEN SERPENT
17 SIGNUM TAU
18 ?

19 DEPOSITION
20 ISAAC CARRYING WOOD
21 SACRIFICE OF ISAAC

22 PELICAN IN HER PIETY
23 ELISHA AND THE SHUNAMMITE'S
    SON
24 WIDOW OF ZAREPHATH
25 BENEDICTION OF JACOB

26 ENTOMBMENT
27 SAMSON AND THE GATES OF
    GAZA
28 DAVID AND THE LION

1-3 DONORS

Fig. 12. Typological Redemption window, Chartres Cathedral, north nave aisle (adapted from Caviness, *Early Glass*). Subjects in small type are modern replacements.

There are other important ways in which windows do not work like books: first, in books the pages have to be turned, and the turning closely shadows the passing of time, so the past is hidden, the present revealed, the future not yet known; there is no "leafing through" a window which may present as many as thirty scenes to a single viewing position; and usually several such windows may be viewed, more or less completely, at once. It is thus easier in windows to create relationships between type scenes—for instance, in the Sainte Chapelle between the many coronations of the Old Testament that culminate in Christ crowned with thorns. And whether their effects were planned or not, the juxtapositions that resulted are how the windows were seen or "recited." Nor could the order of these be predetermined—there is no control of movement patterns through a building, nor of the eyes over a window surface.

Second, as I have already hinted, windows do not usually read like pages of a book, from the top left in rows, but almost always from the bottom up (like a triumphal column). The obvious advantage is that a saint can exit to heaven more conveniently. But we will see that within the frame the sequences may be quite irregular. Furthermore, the normative "bottom up" order can be completely inverted for a reason—as in earlier monumental programs, such as the Hildesheim doors of circa 1000 AD, where the creation and fall move downward on the left valve and the incarnation and redemption move upward on the right.[32]

Finally, my survey has indicated that the narratives most often expand upon the events described in the Vulgate. And here the question may be raised to what extent this reflects apocryphal and vernacular texts of the stories, and to what extent it may be a direct response to the need to fill large Gothic

---

[32] Peter Lasko, *Ars Sacra 800–1200* (Harmondsworth, 1972), 118, pl. 111. This narrative pattern has been referred to as a diptych struture, or "bipartite writing," by William W. Ryding, *Structure in Medievel Narrative*, De proprietatibus Series Major 12 (The Hague, 1971), 40–43. At Canterbury, where the normal reading, most unusually, is top-down, the Redemption Window reverses this in order to follow Christ upward through his resurrection and ascension to his throne in heaven.

windows. The glazing programs reviewed here were created in a period in which the vernacular epic flourished; it may not be mere coincidence that these monuments belong to a crucial phase of architectural development that resulted in enormously enlarged window openings, and consequently greatly increased surfaces over which to expand narrative cycles. To some extent glazing was adapted to the larger size of the window openings in lower stories by adding more narrative medallions, though the panel size was also increased because the glass was generally set higher up than before: at Saint-Denis there were between five and twenty-two subjects in each light; in the typological windows of about 1175–1180 in Canterbury Cathedral there were between fourteen and twenty-one subjects, whereas about 1210–1215 the Becket miracles in the Trinity Chapel filled sixteen to thirty-three compositions in narrower lights; at Chartres between eighteen and thirty-six historiated scenes are included in lancets half as tall again as those of Saint-Denis.[33] *A priori*, it is as easy to expand a story in pictures as to do it in words; and it is as likely that an expanded vernacular version represents a "recitation" of a cycle in a window, as that the window depends on such a pre-existing text. When primacy is hard to establish, it may be preferable to refer to textual affiliates rather than textual sources.

The typological Redemption Window in the north nave aisle of Chartres, glazed about a decade after the fire of 1194, provides a good example of the star composition to be read without the help of inscriptions (fig. 12).[34] The dominant square panels in the central field control the downward flow of the

---

[33] The Saint-Denis windows are ca. 5.25m. in height, the panels about 50cm.; dimensions are given in Grodecki, *Vitraux de Saint-Denis*. The Canterbury typological windows, which were not enlarged after the fire of 1174, average a little more than 5m. in height, and the panels 70cm.; the Trinity Chapel lancets, 7m. high, have panels up to 80cm. high. Detailed measurements are in Caviness, *Windows*, passim. The lower lancets at Chartres are about 7.5m. high, with panels measuring about 80cm.

[34] Restorations in the upper part largely follow earlier drawings of the original panels, so they are authentic as far as the subjects are concerned.

gospel events, the Carrying of the Cross, the Crucifixion, the Deposition, and the Entombment appearing as a sequence of devotional images; the scenes surrounding them are subsidiary. There is a radical shift from the earlier and more scholarly programs in the Benedictine abbeys in that an armature that would allow for six types to each antitype in fact is used in part to supplement the narrative of the passion itself—as in the scene of Christ carrying the cross, where the side panels have sorrowing women and a group of men with a ladder, and the next two (panels 9 and 10) expand the Passion with a Flagellation and Mocking. Also, Old Testament events are less used as types than in the comparable Canterbury window; bestiary imagery and personifications of Ecclesia and Synagoga supplement Old Testament types for the Crucifixion.[35]

In several of the collections of windows reviewed above Old Testament stories, however, were not without appeal isolated from a fuller biblical context. Joseph cycles were especially popular, and comparison of some of these proves valuable on a number of counts.[36] They provide an astonishing variety in terms of arrangement within windows and narrative order, and also in terms of narrative details, emphases, and invited interpretations. The Vulgate account is in Genesis 37–46 but comparison with this text generally indicates that the glass cycles are apocryphal. The popularity of pictorial cycles going back to at least the sixth century (for instance, in the Vienna Genesis) indicates that embellished sources were available as models before the vernacular translations of the thirteenth century.[37]

---

[35] The Canterbury east window and the Chartres Redemption Window are compared in Caviness, *Early Glass*, appendix, figs. 20–21.

[36] The prevalence of this subject was also noted in English manuscripts in the paper by Nigel Morgan published in this volume. I am grateful to him for discussing a number of points of iconography. It has been surmised that a play of Joseph or *Ordo Joseph* was performed on the third Sunday in lent, when the lesson at matins included most of the Joseph story: Karl Young, ed., *A Liturgical Play of Joseph and his Brethren* (Baltimore, 1911), 1; cf. also K. Young, *The Drama of the Medieval Church* (Oxford, 1962), 2:266–76, 485–86.

[37] Useful surveys of the development of Joseph iconography are Pierre Fabre, "Le développement de l'histoire de Joseph dans la littéra-

At the Chartres, the star pattern of the armature invites centering of certain scenes, and the diagonal placement of others allows an upward reading that is almost serpentine or boustrophedon in order. The accompanying figure indicates the sequence of events by a continuous arrow, while short arrows indicate the movement of figures which help the direction of the narrative (figs. 13, 14, 15). The outward journey of Joseph's brothers (fig. 15, and panel 19) is reversed when they come home (panels 23 a–c), a convention already used for the holy family in the mid-twelfth-century Infancy window of the west facade. Gestures or connector figures indicate continuity of the action beyond the frames. Other visual clues, in a complex story with a large cast, include repetition of figure types, such as a Jacob in profile and a Joseph who maintains his young appearance regardless of the passing of time. Coincidence with the Vulgate text appears close at first, since the lowest armature division comprises a complete chapter of Genesis; but three chapters are compressed into the next division, with a right-left reversal of chapters 40 and 41. In the center of the third section (19a and b) two of the brothers' journeys are conflated; or the sequence could be viewed twice, as if movie footage had been repeated. The culminating scene is of the greeting of Jacob by Joseph (25), couched in terms of parental reconciliation rather than homage, and therefore not dream-fulfilling, as in the text.

The centered subjects tend to be symmetrical; they highlight the prophetic dreams, Joseph's posture at the opening of the story reiterated three panels up by Pharaoh dreaming (fig. 15, 3 and 15b). Joseph's trials fall between: peripheral scenes are full of turmoil, as he leaves home to watch the flocks and is sold to passing merchants, but in an ordered composition in the center

---

ture et dans l'art au cours des douze premiers siècles," *Mélanges d'Archéologie et d'Histoire* (Ecole française de Rome) 39 (1921–22): 193–211, who however perhaps overemphasizes the Christological interpretation given to Joseph; and U. Nilgen, "Joseph von Aegypten," in *Lexikon der christlichen Ikonographie: Allgemeine Ikonographie* (Rome, 1970), 2:423–31. For apocryphal subjects in the Vienne Genesis cycle, see Michael D. Levin, "Some Jewish Sources of the Vienna Genesis," *Art Bulletin* 44 (1972): 241–44.

he is lowered into the pit (and/or lifted from it), events that were sometimes taken as foreshadowing the entombment and resurrection of Christ. In the center of the next division (10) he resists the advances of Potiphar's wife, who symbolizes unchastity; his trial and imprisonment are peripheral. After Pharaoh dreaming, the next central scene is the Egyptians pouring chaff into the river Nile; apocryphal vernacular texts explain that this was done so that Joseph's father would see it downstream and know there was grain in Egypt during the famine (18). This event curiously displaces the biblical subject of storing the grain (17), but the prominence given to it here is mirrored in the Bourges and Rouen cycles and it deserves further attention below, especially since it has never been correctly identified in the glass. There follows, in axis, the feast during which Joseph sits apart from his brothers, and their return home which breaks the rule of symmetry (21 and 23b); an image of Christ in majesty presides over the whole cycle, displacing the culminating greeting of father and son to the side (26 and 25).

It is noteworthy that this telling of a tale of individual trials and of family betrayals and reunions has a parallel in a window just around the corner of the transept which treats the parable of the prodigal son. Departure from a loving father, in the bottom section in each case, is followed by temptations and near ruin; feasting and reunion at the end of the story are presided over by the Almighty. Both protagonists are studies in filial piety and both epitomize a moral struggle, but whereas Joseph always triumphs over evil and adversity, the prodigal son falls from grace and has to seek forgiveness. Seen on this level, the scholarly lines drawn between Old and New Testament stories, and even hagiography, appear false, and to the audience of the thirteenth century the use of contemporary costume would also serve to dissolve historical distinctions. The association also points up the number of times that Joseph windows were next to or opposite from parables: at Bourges (opposite the Good and Bad Rich Men, with a Good Samaritan and Prodigal Son also in the ambulatory), at Poitiers (facing the Prodigal Son in the transepts), at Rouen (facing the Good Samaritan), at Auxerre (across from the Prodigal son).

The contemporary Bourges window, a gift of the wheel-

Fig. 13. Joseph Window, lower half, Chartres Cathedral, north nave aisle (after Delaporte and Houvet, *Les Vitraux de Chartres*).

Fig. 14. Joseph Window, upper half, Chartres Cathedral, north nave aisle (after Delaporte and Houvet, *Les Vitraux de Chartres*).

26: MAJESTY

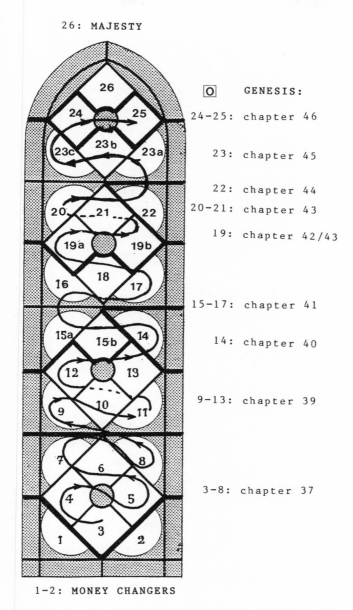

Fig. 15. Diagram of the Chartres Joseph Window, showing the direction of the narrative and of movement (the author).

Fig. 16. Joseph Window, Bourges Cathedral, ambulatory of the choir 25 (after Cahier and Martin, *Bourges*).

wrights, was disordered when Cahier and Martin drew it (fig.
16); the central scenes above that with Joseph's dream in the
bottom, are confused and the two losenges with the chaff scene
and the merchant buying Joseph should be switched. The
composition somewhat resembles that of the Chartres window,
but there are fewer compartments and the cycle is condensed,
leaving out the feast and the cup hidden in the brothers' sacks,
and abbreviating the journeying of the brothers; the reunion is
with Benjamin rather than Jacob in the summit.

The astonishing thing about each of these Joseph cycles is that
no two are alike; even though one Rouen window has the
signature of a painter called Clement of Chartres, he does not
reproduce the chartrain narrative (fig. 19). Instead, he spreads
twice as many subjects through two lancets, beginning from the
top of the first and tracing a descent (as in the Hildesheim door)
to the imprisonment (fig. 17–19). His ascendance begins at the
bottom of the pendant window (where the drapers are represented as donors), with the baker and butler in prison, through
Joseph's rise to power in the famine, and ending as at Chartres
with the greeting of Jacob (figs. 20–22).

At Poitiers, on the other hand, though the first window
begins from the top and traces the events down to Joseph sold
by his brothers, the opportunity to begin upwards in the second
half is missed; the second window begins at the top with his
entry into Potiphar's service, and ends with the family reunion
in the bottom (fig. 5).

Auxerre, with a register missing at the bottom, now begins
with the stripping of Joseph's cloak by his brothers, and reads
predominantly right to left, with some reversals in the Potiphar
sequence that might be partly due to misplaced panels.[38] One
remarkable aspect of this cycle is the child-like stature of Joseph
throughout (figs. 23–24). Another is in its culmination: rather
than pursuing the story to the reunion with his family, the cycle
ends with Joseph riding in the chariot Pharaoh gave him. The
chariot, absent from the contemporary windows, is commoner
in manuscripts, such as the *Bible moralisée*, and the French

---

[38] Raguin, *Burgundy*, 147–48.

Fig. 17. First Joseph Window, top section (beginning with his dream), Rouen Cathedral, ambulatory of the choir 16 (after Ritter, *Les Vitraux*).

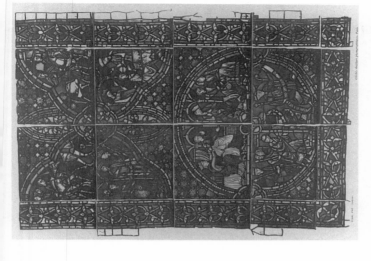

Fig. 18. First Joseph Window, mid section, Rouen Cathedral, ambulatory of the choir 16 (after Ritter, *Les Vitraux*).

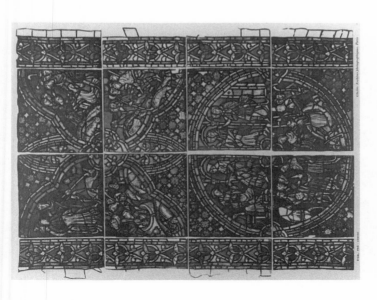

Fig. 19. First Joseph Window, bottom section (ending with the painter's signature, Clement of Chartres), Rouen Cathedral, ambulatory of the choir 16 (after Ritter, *Les Vitraux*).

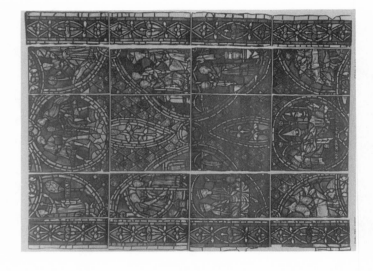

Fig. 21. Second Joseph Window, mid section, Rouen Cathedral, ambulatory of the choir 17 (after Ritter, *Les Vitraux*).

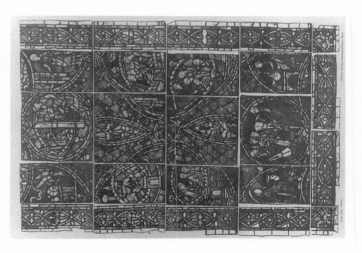

Fig. 20. Second Joseph Window, bottom section (donors and prison scenes), Rouen Cathedral, ambulatory of the choir 17 (after Ritter, *Les Vitraux*).

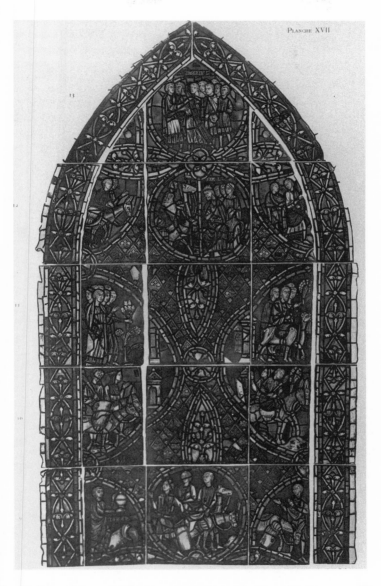

Fig. 22. Second Joseph Window, top section (closing with the reconcilia-tion), Rouen Cathedral, ambulatory of the choir 17 (after Ritter, *Les Vitraux*).

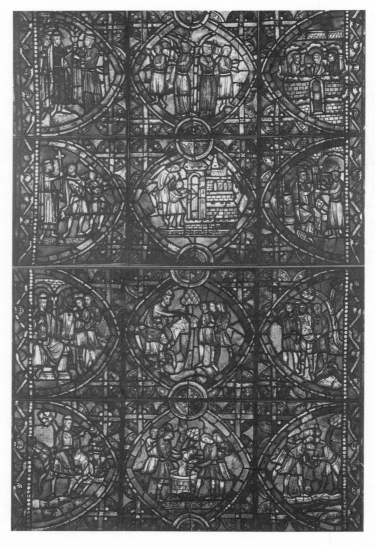

Fig. 23. Joseph Window, lower half (incomplete at the bottom), Auxerre Cathedral, ambulatory of the choir 53 (photo: S.P.A.D.E.M.).

Fig. 24. Joseph Window, upper half (incomplete at the top), Auxerre Cathedral, ambulatory of the choir 53 (photo: S.P.A.D.E.M.).

Histoire universelle.[39] Earlier theologians had associated Joseph's chariot with the quadriga drawn by the evangelist symbols that was described in the vision of Amminadab, as illustrated in the *Bibles moralisées*.[40] The thrust of the Auxerre cycle seems to be ecclesiastic, presenting Joseph as a type of the priesthood, as in the early ivories on the throne of Maximian in

[39] Dorothy W. Gillerman, *The Clôture of Notre-Dame and its Role in the Fourteenth-Century Choir Program* (New York, 1977), 82–92 and fig. 69 (a Parisian recension of the Histoire Universelle dating ca. 1300, Paris, Bibliothèque Nationale MS. fr. 20125).

[40] A. de Laborde, *La bible moralisée illustrée* (Paris, 1911–29), pl. 674 (Vienna, cod. 1179 f. 23v).

Ravenna as well as in the lost thirteenth-century relief sculptures from the choir closure of Notre-Dame in Paris.[41]

The Sainte Chapelle cycle is the last to be mentioned, but its very heavy restoration in the nineteenth century makes judgements quite uncertain. It should be emphasized that Joseph, unlike Esther and Judith, is not singled out as a "hero" for separate treatment; he simply takes his place in the Genesis sequence, in twenty scenes of the top four registers of the first window on the north side (fig. 8, window O). But the scenes of reunion spill over into the tracery above, and into the authentically preserved tracery of the next bay (N), giving them an air of sanctity; the patriarch's death is represented in the very summit.[42] A similar cycle exists in fragmentary state in Tours Cathedral.[43]

This survey has scarcely done justice to the varied details of these Joseph cycles, but one apocryphal scene is worth returning to briefly because its visual emphasis in three of the windows, at the expense of the biblical version of the event, raises certain problems of interpretation. This is the scene of Egyptians pouring chaff into the Nile which is centrally placed in the Bourges, Chartres, and Rouen windows (figs. 14, 16, 21, 25, 26, 27). The Vulgate recounts simply that Joseph, having interpreted the Pharaoh's dream that the seven years of plenty would be followed by as many years of famine, ordered the surplus grain to be stored in the city and gave it out to the people in the lean years; Jacob, in his distant homeland, heard of the availability of grain in Egypt and sent his sons to buy there (Genesis 41.29–57 and 42.1–3). A biblical poem in French, composed by Herman, a canon of Valenciennes in the twelfth century, included Joseph's signal to Jacob by ordering the straw to be thrown into the Nile so that it would be seen in Jerusalem(!).[44] There are

----

[41] Meyer Schapiro, "The Joseph Scenes of the Maximianus Throne in Ravenna," *Gazette des Beaux-Arts* 40 (1952): 27–38; Gillerman, *Notre-Dame*, 96; the closure, however, was also Christological.

[42] Aubert, *Vitraux de Paris*, pls. 14–15, 20–21.

[43] Studied by Linda Papanicolaou, "Stained Glass Windows of the Choir of the Cathedral of Tours" (Ph.D. diss., New York University, 1979), 129–34, pls. 99–101.

[44] J. Bonnard, *Les Traductions de la Bible en vers français au Moyen Age*

Fig. 25. Joseph directing the chaff to be thrown in the River Nile so that Jacob might see it, Rouen, detail of fig. 21.

later English texts that incorporate this anecdote, as well as representations in other media, but the import seems purely narrative.[45] The Rouen window gives the fullest and clearest rendering of this episode: Joseph, in a cap and with his newly bestowed mace or scepter (replacing the gold chain and ring that

---

(Paris, 1884), 15; Herman's identity is given on 11, 38–41. One of the twenty-one manuscripts known to Bonnard was at Chartres (MS. 261). I have examined the oldest manuscript mentioned by Bonnard, Paris, Bibliothèque Nationale MS. fr. 2162, which looks to be twelfth-century. The Joseph legend is on fols. 15–25ᵛ, with the chaff episode ("la paille de ces bles est en laigue iectee") on fol. 20. Cf. also MS. fr. 1444, fol. 15ᵛ.

[45] A French thirteenth-century Psalter, formerly Dyson Perrins MS. 32, now in Santa Monica, The Getty Museum, MS. Ludwig VIII, 4, f. 18, includes the episode. So also do the Salisbury sculptures; see Pamela Z. Blum, "The Middle English Romance 'Iacob and Iosep' and the Joseph Cycle of the Salisbury Chapter House," *Gesta* 8 (1969): 25, fig. 11. For the text followed there, a mid-century metrical poem, see Arthur S. Napier, ed., *Iacob and Iosep: A Middle English Poem of the Thirteenth Century* (Oxford, 1916), 11 (the text, however, is incomplete at this point, but refers to chaff found by Jacob's sons). The episode is also in the *Cursor Mundi: A Northumbrian Poem of the Fourteenth Century*, ed. Richard Morris (London, 1961), part 1, 278; I am grateful to Nigel Morgan for this reference.

Fig. 26. Joseph directing the chaff to be thrown in the River Nile, Bourges (photo: S.P.A.D.E.M.).

Fig. 27. The chaff thrown in the River Nile and the grain stored in the cities, Chartres, detail of fig. 14.

are specified in the Vulgate as his insignia), raises his arm in command on the left, while two agricultural workers pour the chaff into the turbulent river in the center; Jacob, with one son, observes it floating by them, on the right (fig. 25). In the single scene at Bourges, Joseph also stands on the left, and here the grain storage is referred to behind him, but there are no witnesses (fig. 26). At Chartres the storing of grain is separated to the right, but Joseph is not shown directing these activities (fig. 27). In each case, however, the chaff scene is not only central but has a symmetrical composition that gives it great solemnity. As ever with medieval art, it is easier to speculate what the meaning might have been for the learned than for the unlearned: the parable of the harvest clearly suggested that the wheat and the chaff would be separated at the Last Judgement, the grain to be stored in the (heavenly) city, the straw to be burned (in hell), and this had been represented in one of the Canterbury typological windows.[46] Joseph, then, is a type of the Judge, and this seems to match his dress and behavior in Bourges and Rouen; but why should damnation be emphasized over salvation? The answer might well lie in the trials of heretics and the increasing pressure on the Jews to convert to Christianity in the early thirteenth century; in earlier glosses Joseph's brothers were seen as the Jews, the Egyptians who accepted him more readily as the gentiles.[47] The chaff tossed into the river is a warning, as well as a promise, to the people of Jacob. Yet it could not have been interpreted without verbal aid.

My conclusions must be brief: to the general notion that the cathedral programs of the thirteenth century were dominated by a passion for storytelling, and that few biblical windows were based on the Vulgate alone, this detailed digression has added the insight that each story could be told in pictures many times over without dull repetition, and with a variety of encoded messages. The time is too late in the development of rich

---

[46] Caviness, *Windows*, 126; this sixth window began with the parable of the sower and ended with the feeding of the five thousand, i.e., the distribution of bread.

[47] As also in the Canterbury glass; Caviness, *Windows*, 94–95, fig. 165.

apocryphal pictorial cycles, let alone the textual variants, for it to be very fruitful to play with stemma, and if texts were available at all they were likely vernacular expansions of the story with some moralizing asides. These traits led Bonnard to characterize Herman's poem as "une chanson de geste ecclésiastique." In this period texts and pictures have equal autonomy; in fact windows (since they are public) are as likely to have influenced vernacular texts as the other way. Once independent of a text, the window stands by itself and is open to variant readings and interpretations that need not be "corrected" in reference to a text; the ordering of events also varies in the verbal narratives. Indeed, a modern view of history (as in Robbe-Grillet) provides no canonical sequence, only an infinite variety of experiences and memories to be registered by an audience in light of their own experience. Some insight into this process may be gained from a story that was popular along the pilgrim routes, as reported by Marilyn Stokstad: A boy rejected the advances of a girl at an inn; in revenge she hid two silver cups in his pouch, and then denounced him for stealing; he was hanged, but his parents found him alive on their return from Santiago, saved by their prayers to St. James.[48] It is easy to imagine a Joseph cycle supplying these events, in the form of Joseph and Potiphar's wife and the accusation, the cup hidden in the brother's baggage, the hanging of the baker, and the reconciliation of the family—if the "reading" involved confabulation on the basis of pictorial imagery.

Each Joseph window was to be read in its own context. For a somewhat sophisticated audience, Joseph could be a figure for Christ (but this is seldom explicit in the glass cycles), for the priesthood (on the screen of Notre-Dame and at Auxerre perhaps, but not overtly in a window connected with an artisan corporation), for a faithful steward, well rewarded (in a king's manuscript, such as the *Bible moralisée*, and chapel), and (in the cathedrals) for a younger son in a feudal society that was in the process, around 1200, of adapting to patrilineage, with much

---

[48] Marilyn Stokstad, *Santiago de Compostela in the Age of Great Pilgrimages* (Norman, OK, 1978), 29.

hardship for younger sons who sometimes had little inheritance.[49] He was also a figure for younger sons who departed to the Holy Land to earn a fortune; for a freed man, a visionary, and an overseer. The temptations of Potiphar's wife (a king's wife in many versions, including Herman's) would be more poignantly seen in the context of the insistence on chastity by the Cathars. A moral man who rose up from servitude to great success is a sufficient role model for laics, such as drapers, wheelwrights, and money changers, who could thus associate their trade with sacred history. I tend to see these windows indeed as Bibles of the laity, but it is a Bible transformed into popular romance, more vividly reflecting contemporary sociological structures than esoteric spiritual truths. Even the contemporary costume of the protagonists was an equalizer. My attempt to classify the windows of Chartres according to different divisions of history—though this is clear in earlier monastic programs such as St. Denis and Canterbury—does not work. There is ultimately no distinction between heroes.

---

[49] David Herlihy, *Medieval Households* (Cambridge, MA, 1985), 95–97, 136–38.

Old Testament Illustration in Thirteenth-Century England

Nigel Morgan

In memory of Hanns Swarzenski

Just over fifty years ago the late Hanns Swarzenski published for the first time the series of Bible pictures by the English artist William de Brailes in MS. W.106 in the Walters Art Gallery, Baltimore.[1] In this article he discussed the Old Testament miniatures which preface several English Psalters of the thirteenth century, making a series of perceptive comments on the interrelationships between the various manuscripts. A problem not resolved in his study was the individual and frequently idiosyncratic choice of subjects chosen for illustration. It is this problem which will be examined in this paper, both in relation to manuscript illumination and to monumental cycles in wall painting and sculpture.

The illustration of the Old Testament had of course been long established as a tradition in England by the thirteenth century. In the eleventh century there had been extensive illustration of Caedmon's Genesis and Aelfric's Hexateuch.[2] In these manu-

---

[1] H. Swarzenski, "Unknown Bible Pictures by W. de Brailes and Some Notes on Early English Bible Illustration," *Journal of the Walters Art Gallery* 1 (1938): 55–69.

[2] See I. Gollancz, *The Caedmon Manuscript* (Oxford, 1927), and C. R. Dodwell and P. Clemoes, *The Old English Illustrated Hexateuch: British Museum Cotton Claudius B.IV* (Copenhagen, 1974), for facsimiles with commentary. For the Caedmon manuscript see in addition G. D. S. Henderson, "The Programme of Illustrations in Bodleian MS Junius XI," in *Studies in Memory of David Talbot Rice*, ed. G. Robertson and G.

scripts vernacular paraphrases of the biblical text were illustrated by numerous drawings whose iconography often follows the
narrative of the Anglo-Saxon text rather than that of the Vulgate. It is a matter of controversy whether the artists used older
pictorial cycles as models, or whether, for the most part, they
directly illustrated the text they had before them.[3] In the
twelfth century there is no clear evidence of any continuation of
such illustrated vernacular paraphrases, which would at that
time no longer have been in Anglo-Saxon, but in Anglo-Norman French. An extensive series of Old and New Testament
scenes, now isolated leaves, may once have prefaced the mid-
twelfth-century Canterbury copy of the Utrecht Psalter (Cambridge, Trinity Coll. MS. R.17.1), and this is an early instance,
with that of the Winchester Psalter (London, British Library MS.
Cotton Nero C.IV), of the use of such Old Testament pictures
before Psalters.[4] The sources of the pictures and the reason for

---

Henderson (Edinburgh, 1975), 113–42. For a recent annotated bibliography of studies on both manuscripts see R. Deshman, *Anglo-Saxon and
Anglo-Scandinavian Art: An Annotated Bibliography* (Boston, 1984), 18–25.

[3] See in particular the discussion in Dodwell and Clemoes, *Illustrated
Hexateuch*, 65–73, and the comments by Deshman in his annotated
bibliography. A discussion of the two manuscripts in relation to the
Early Christian cycle of the Cotton Genesis is given in K. Weitzmann
and H. L. Kessler, *The Cotton Genesis* (Princeton, 1986), passim. For
discussion of the supposed influence of this Early Christian/Anglo-
Saxon cycle on later works see G. D. S. Henderson, "Late Antique
Influences in Some English Medieval Illustrations of Genesis," *Journal of
the Warburg and Courtauld Institutes* 25 (1962): 172–98; G. D. S. Henderson, "The Sources of the Genesis Cycle at Saint-Savin-sur-Gartempe,"
Journal of the British Archaeological Association, ser. 3, 26 (1963): 11–26; and
the studies by Kristine Haney cited in n. 4.

[4] M. R. James, "Four Leaves of an English Psalter of the Twelfth
Century," *Walpole Society* 25 (1936/37): 1–32; C. R. Dodwell, *The Canter-
bury School of Illumination 1066–1200* (Cambridge, 1954), 99–102; A.
Heimann, "The Last Copy of the Utrecht Psalter," in *The Year 1200: A
Symposium, the Metropolitan Museum of Art, New York*, ed. J. Hoffeld
(New York, 1975), 317–20; and *English Romanesque Art 1066–1200*,
Exhibition, Hayward Gallery, London, 1984, no. 47, for the leaves which
may have prefaced the copy of the Utrecht Psalter. F. Wormald, *The
Winchester Psalter* (London, 1973), 14–17, 69–70, plates 5–10; K. E. Haney,
"Some Old Testament Pictures in the Psalter of Henry of Blois," *Gesta*
24/1(1985): 33–45; and K. E. Haney, *The Winchester Psalter: An Iconogra-*

the choice of subjects of the former remains to be elucidated. Kristine Haney has recently made some perceptive suggestions concerning the scenes included in the Winchester Psalter, connecting the choice of subject matter with the matins readings from Septuagesima Sunday to the Fourth Sunday in Lent.[5] This reading of the Old Testament stories from Adam and Eve to Moses in the Breviary during this season of the church year is an important influence, although for most cycles the readings only partly correspond to the choice of subjects.

From the closing years of the twelfth century biblical paraphrases become popular, and continue, both in Latin and the vernacular, as an important genre for the rest of the Middle Ages. The *Historia scholastica* of Petrus Comestor, not strictly speaking a paraphrase, as it contains so much commentary, is part of this rise of selective presentation of the biblical text.[6] Its influence is constantly found in the paraphrases which followed

---

phic Study (Leicester, 1986), 53–57, 76–92 for the Winchester Psalter. The manuscripts are also discussed at length in C. M. Kauffmann, *Romanesque Manuscripts 1066–1190, Survey of Manuscripts Illuminated in the British Isles* (London, 1975), vol. 3, nos. 66, 78.

In addition to these examples in manuscript illumination an important cycle of Old Testament scenes is in the sculpture of the archivolts of the portal of Malmesbury Abbey: K. J. Galbraith, "The Iconography of the Biblical Scenes at Malmesbury Abbey," *Journal of the British Archaeological Association* 28 (1965): 39–56; P. Strohm, "The Malmesbury Medallions and Twelfth Century Typology," *Mediaeval Studies* 33 (1971): 180–87. Also of the middle years of the twelfth century were the paintings, now lost, of the choir enclosure of the Abbey of Bury St. Edmunds: M. R. James, *On the Abbey of St. Edmund at Bury* (Cambridge, 1895), 200–202. An Anglo-Saxon Psalter, London, British Library MS. Cotton Tiberius C.VI places a series of David scenes before a New Testament sequence of pictures preceding the Psalter, and is the earliest example in England of such illustrations set before the Psalter: F. Wormald, "An English Eleventh-Century Psalter with Pictures," *Walpole Society* 38 (1962): 1–13, with a complete series of plates of the illustrations.

[5] Haney, *Winchester Psalter*, 54–57.

[6] The only modern edition which exists of the text is in Migne, *Patrologia Latina* (1885), 198.1054–1722. For the author see S. L. Daly, "Peter Comestor: Master of Histories," *Speculum* 32 (1957): 62–73; D. Luscombe, "Peter Comestor," in *The Bible in the Medieval World. Essays in Memory of Beryl Smalley,* ed. K. Walsh and D. Wood (Oxford, 1985), 109–29.

its choice of subject matter and extracted its extra-biblical detail. Of equal importance is the *Aurora* of Peter of Riga, a versified and highly selective Bible paraphrase with theological commentary.[7] These books were to become fundamental reference books for the rest of the Middle Ages. A third work, the *Compendium historiae in genealogia Christi* of Peter of Poitiers, was of equivalent influence.[8] Its brief biographical entries on biblical figures provide a concise listing of the main events in their lives. In the French vernacular, a work evidently much read in England, in view of surviving manuscripts of English provenance, was the *Romanz de Dieu et de Sa Mère* by Herman of Valenciennes, written during the last quarter of the twelfth century.[9] The influence of this work can be seen in the three Middle English thirteenth-century paraphrases, the Genesis and Exodus, *Iacob and Iosep*, and the *Cursor Mundi*.[10] The first two

---

[7] This is now in an excellent recent edition: P. E. Beichner, *Aurora Petri Rigae Biblia Versificata*, 2 vols. (Notre Dame, 1965).

[8] P. S. Moore, *The Works of Peter of Poitiers* (Notre Dame, 1936); W. Monroe, "A Roll-Manuscript of Peter of Poitiers Compendium," *Bulletin of the Cleveland Museum of Art* 65 (1978): 92–107; H.-E. Hilpert, "Geistliche Bildung und Laienbildung: Zur Überlieferung der Schulschrift *Compendium historiae in genealogia Christi* (Compendium veteris testamenti) des Petrus von Poitiers in England," *Journal of Medieval History* 11 (1985): 315–32. In the latter article the large number of texts listed attests to its popularity in England. For rather innaccurate printed texts of the Compendium see U. Zwingli, *Petri Pictaviensis Galli genealogia et chronologia sanctorum patrum* (Basel, 1592); H. Vollmer, *Deutsche Bibelauszüge des Mittelalters zum Stammbaum Christi* (Potsdam, 1931), 127–87. A modern critical edition is much needed.

[9] An excellent edition has recently been published: I. Spiele, *Li Romanz de Dieu et de Sa Mère d'Herman de Valenciennes* (Leiden, 1975). An earlier study with discussion of sources is F. Mehne, *Inhalt und Quellen der Bible des Herman de Valenciennes* (Halle, 1900). An early manuscript (Phillipps 16378) of English provenance dating from the last quarter of the twelfth century was sold at Sotheby's , November 30, 1976, lot 859. Spiele, *Li Romanz*, 144–54, 158–59, lists the manuscripts of English origin. For the date of composition see A. de Mandach, "A quand remonte la Bible de Herman de Valenciennes," in *Valenciennes et les anciens Pays-Bas, Mélanges offerts à Paul Lefrancq* (Valenciennes, 1976), 53–69.

[10] For Middle English Genesis and Exodus see R. Morris, *The Story of Genesis and Exodus*, Early English Text Society, o.s., 7 (1865); O. Arngart, *The Middle English Genesis and Exodus* (Lund, 1968); A. Fritz-

date from the first half of the century, and the monumental *Cursor Mundi* from the last quarter. These paraphrases have not come down to us in extensively illustrated manuscripts, and it is very unlikely that they ever received cycles of pictures. It is in the prefatory miniatures of the Psalters and monumental wall painting and sculpture that Old Testament illustration has survived, and it is these forms of art that provide clear evidence that artists, or their advisors or patrons, were well acquainted with these paraphrases. Although these Old Testament illustrations are separated from any textual context, excepting those which have Anglo-Norman *tituli*, their choice of subject, as will be shown, has close parallels with that of the paraphrases. It does not seem that there is direct influence from any particular text, but rather that the picture cycles provide visual equivalents to the paraphrases, which must have been used as reference books in their planning.

The illustration of the Latin Bible itself, in which historiated initials are placed at the beginning of each of the books, may have some relevance to the narrative cycles in the Psalters, wall paintings, and sculpture, but if this is the case it is not immediately apparent.[11] With the single exception of the Lothian Bible

---

sche, "Ist die altenglische 'Story of Genesis and Exodus' das Werk eines Verfassers?" *Anglia* 5 (1882): 43–90. For *Iacob and Iosep* see A. S. Napier, *Iacob and Iosep: A Middle English Poem of the Thirteenth Century* (Oxford, 1916); O. Sherwin, "Art's Spring-Birth: The Ballad of Iacob and Iosep," *Studies in Philology* 42 (1945): 1–18. For *Cursor Mundi* see R. Morris, *Cursor Mundi*, Early English Text Society, o.s., 57, 59, 62, 66, 68, 99, 101 (1874–93); H. C. W. Haenisch, *Inquiry into the Sources of the Cursor Mundi*, Early English Text Society, o.s., 99 (1892), 1–56 (this section was not printed in the reprint edition); L. Borland, "Herman's Bible and the Cursor Mundi," *Studies in Philology* 30 (1933): 427–44; P. E. Beichner, "The Cursor Mundi and Petrus Riga," *Speculum* 24 (1949): 239–50; P. Buehler, "The Cursor Mundi and Herman's Bible—Some Additional Parallels," *Studies in Philology* 61 (1964): 485–98; E. Mardon, *The Narrative Unity of the Cursor Mundi* (Glasgow, 1970); S. M. Horrall, "An Old French Source for the Genesis Section of Cursor Mundi," *Mediaeval Studies* 40 (1978): 361–73; S. M. Horrall, *The Southern Version of Cursor Mundi*, vol. 1 (Ottawa, 1978). There is a good general discussion of these Middle English texts in D. C. Fowler, *The Bible in Early English Literature* (Seattle, 1976), 127–32, 134–40, 165–93.

[11] For English thirteenth-century Bibles with historiated initials see

the subjects chosen for the historiated initials mostly differ from those found in the Old Testament cycles.[12] The choice of subject tends to be conventional, although, if alternatives exist, artists of a single workshop may vary the scene for their various products.[13] Throughout the century there is influence from French Bible illustration, and it is difficult to assess the situation in England until the French material is better published. The individual case of the Lothian Bible requires explanation, for a series of narrative scenes are placed in the initials at the beginning of some of the books.

The Old Testament illustrations preceding Psalters at first appearance seem to present a series of briefly depicted Bible stories of the main figures: Adam and Eve, Cain and Abel, Noah, Abraham and Lot, Isaac, Jacob and Joseph, Moses, Ruth, Samuel, and David. Some of the scenes depicted have typological significance as prefigurations of the life of Christ, but this is in no way clarified for the onlooker by the use of inscriptions, as is usual in works of typological art. In the second half of the twelfth century such typological programs are usually accompanied by those inscriptions in leonine hexameters so loved by twelfth-century versifiers. At Canterbury, in the glass, and at Worcester, and at Peterborough in wall paintings now lost, such elaborate schemes were set up.[14] The possibly Cistercian au-

---

N. Morgan, *Early Gothic Manuscripts 1190–1250, Survey of Manuscripts Illuminated in the British Isles*, vol. 4, part 1 (Oxford, 1982), nos. 32, 58, 62, 63, 65, 66, 69, 70, 75 and N. Morgan, *Early Gothic Manuscripts 1250–1285, Survey of Manuscripts Illuminated in the British Isles*, vol. 4, part 2 (London, 1988), nos. 102, 105, 135, 139, 142, 143, 148, 159, 163, 164, 168, 169, 170, 180. A fundamental study of English thirteenth-century Bibles is A. Bennett, "The Place of Garrett 28 in Thirteenth-Century English Illumination" (Ph.D diss., Columbia University, 1973).

[12] For the Lothian Bible see Morgan, *Early Gothic Manuscripts 1190–1250*, no. 32, and J. Plummer, "The Lothian-Morgan Bible" (Ph.D. diss., Columbia University, 1953).

[13] See Morgan, *Early Gothic Manuscripts 1190–1250*, nos. 62, 63, 65, 66, and *Early Gothic Manuscripts 1250–1285*, nos. 142, 143, 148, 169, 170 for Bibles of the same workshop but with different choices of subjects for the initials.

[14] On Canterbury see M. H. Caviness, *The Early Stained Glass of Canterbury Cathedral* (Princeton, 1977), 115–38. On Worcester see M. R.

thor of the *Pictor in carmine* provides a compendium listing subjects with accompanying verses to assist clerics or artists in the compilation of such programs.[15] The lack of such verse inscriptions for the Old Testament scenes preceding Psalters suggests that if typological allusions were intended they were at a much simpler level.[16] Certain scenes from the earliest days of Christian art had a typological meaning, and assuredly in the thirteenth century most literate people would be aware of such a meaning.[17] These scenes in the Psalters are, however, parts of a series of pictures, the majority of which could not be given a typological interpretation.

There are seven surviving English thirteenth-century Psalters with a series of Old Testament pictures of some length.[18] Several more have a handful of scenes restricted to those of the Creation, Adam and Eve, and Cain and Abel. Of this latter category, the best examples would be the Carrow and Huth Psalters, and the number of scenes is so small that they are in no way comparable with the other seven manuscripts which have from sixteen to 176 pictures.[19] As a parallel to these seven

---

James, "On Two Series of Paintings Formerly at Worcester Priory," *Proceedings of the Cambridge Antiquarian Society* 10 (1900–1901), and N. Stratford, "Three English Romanesque Enamelled Ciboria," *Burlington Magazine* 126 (1984): 204–16. On Peterborough see L. F. Sandler, "Peterborough Abbey and the Peterborough Psalter in Brussels," *Journal of the British Archaeological Association* 33 (1970): 36–49.

[15] M. R. James, "Pictor in Carmine," *Archaeologia* 94 (1951): 141–66.

[16] Where inscriptions exist as in the Huntingfield, De Brailes and St. John's manuscripts they are as simple *tituli* without typological allusion.

[17] For example, the Sacrifice of Cain and Abel, Crossing of the Red Sea, Samson Fighting the Lion as prefigurations of the Sacrifice of Christ, the Baptism, and the Harrowing of Hell.

[18] Morgan, *Early Gothic Manuscripts 1190–1250*, nos. 1, 14, 23, 30, 51, 71; *Early Gothic Manuscripts 1250–1285*, no. 179. See the Appendix at the end of this article for a list of Old Testament subjects in these works arranged according to biblical order. There is also a short Old Testament cycle of some importance in the circa 1265 Oscott Psalter, in the side medallions beside the New Testament scenes (Morgan, *Early Gothic Manuscripts 1250–1285*, no. 151).

[19] The shortest cycle is in the St. John's Psalter and the longest in the Munich Psalter. For the Carrow and Huth Psalters see Morgan, *Early Gothic Manuscripts 1250–1285*, nos. 118, 167.

Psalters three examples survive in monumental art. The earliest is the early thirteenth-century painted decoration by a travelling Winchester artist in the Chapter House of the convent of Sigena in Catalonia, sadly almost completely destroyed in the Spanish Civil War, but the wall paintings were fortunately recorded in an excellent series of photographs taken shortly before their destruction.[20] The twenty Old Testament scenes at Sigena, as in all of the Psalters, are accompanied by a series of scenes of the life of Christ. No typological connection seems intended, and both cycles are in strict narrative order. The Old Testament series has scenes of the Creation, and from the lives of Adam and Eve, Cain and Abel, Noah, Abraham, Moses and David.

In the sculpture of the lower level of the West Front of Wells Cathedral, probably of circa 1230 in date, sixteen Old Testament scenes are set in quatrefoils.[21] The subjects are the Creation, and the lives of Adam and Eve, Cain and Abel, Noah, Isaac(?) and Jacob. Finally circa 1270–1280, also in sculpture, in the Salisbury Chapter House, a large cycle of sixty-five scenes (regrettably much restored in the 1850s), is set in the spandrels of the wall arcade.[22] It contains the Creation, and the lives of Adam and Eve, Cain and Abel, Noah, Abraham and Lot, Isaac, Jacob and Joseph, and Moses.

One of the manuscripts considered to be from a Psalter, the one which had been the subject of Hanns Swarzenski's paper, has no accompanying text and might have been a Bible picture book without text. The suggestion has frequently been made that the pictures once prefaced a Psalter or Book of Hours, but

---

[20] W. Oakeshott, *Sigena: Romanesque Paintings in Spain and the Winchester Bible Artists* (London, 1972). The remains of the Sigena paintings are now in Barcelona, Museum of Catalan Art.

[21] W. H. St. John Hope and W. R. Lethaby, "The Imagery and Sculptures on the West Front of Wells Cathedral Church," *Archaeologia* 59 (1904): 188–91.

[22] W. Burges, "The Iconography of the Chapter-House, Salisbury," *The Ecclesiologist* 20 (1859): 109–62; P. Z. Blum, "The Middle English Romance 'Iacob and Iosep' and the Joseph Cycle of the Salisbury Chapter House," *Gesta* 8 (1969): 18–34; S. Whittingham, *Salisbury Chapter House* (Salisbury, 1979).

it remains only a hypothesis.[23] In France three examples survive of thirteenth-century Bible picture books, and there may have been equivalents in England.[24]

The earliest of the series of Psalters with Old Testament pictures is the so-called Great Canterbury Psalter, the last copy of the Utrecht Psalter, probably dating from shortly before 1200. It stands apart from the other six Psalters in having a triple text of the Gallican, Hebraic, and Roman Psalter with glosses. It is therefore a Psalter whose text is primarily for scholarly study rather than devotion. It is also different from the others in that it is the only one almost certainly made under Benedictine patronage, that of the Cathedral Priory of Christ Church, Canterbury. Finally, its model may be a manuscript of the middle years of the twelfth century, which conditions its choice of subject.[25] If it closely depends on that model, then its program antedates the rise of the biblical paraphrases following the appearance of Petrus Comestor's *Historia scholastica* circa 1169–1175. The format of illustration as a set of twelve scenes to a page, sometimes combining two episodes, arranged as a grid, derives from its mid-twelfth-century predecessor (fig. 1). There are forty-seven scenes in all: the last page ends with the beginning of a New Testament cycle. The scenes are of the Creation, Adam and Eve, Cain and Abel, Noah, Abraham, Jacob and

---

[23] Swarzenski, "Unknown Bible Pictures," 63; P. Brieger, *English Art 1216–1307* (Oxford, 1968), 89.

[24] For Manchester, John Rylands Library MS. fr. 5 see R. Fawtier, *La Bible Historiée toute figurée de la John Rylands Library* (Paris, 1924). For New York, Pierpont Morgan Library, MS. M. 638 see S. C. Cockerell and M. R. James, *A Book of Old Testament Illustrations* (Roxburghe Club, 1926); S. C. Cockerell and J. Plummer, *Old Testament Miniatures* (New York, 1969); H. Stahl, "Old Testament Illustration During the Reign of St. Louis: The Morgan Picture Book and the New Biblical Cycles," *Il Medio Oriente e l'Occidente nell'arte del XIII secolo,* ed. H. Belting, Atti del XXIV Congresso Internazionale di Storia dell'Arte, Bologna, 1979 (Bologna, 1982), 79–93. For Chicago, Art Inst, 15.533 see *The Huth Library, A Catalogue of the Printed Books, Manuscripts, Autograph Letters and Engravings, Collected by Henry Huth* (London, 1880), 1:165–66; *Catalogue of the Huth Collection, Sotheby Sale, November 15th–24th, 1911,* no. 739; *Bulletin of the Art Institute of Chicago,* 16, no. 5 (1922): 75.

[25] See n. 4 for references.

Joseph, Moses, Joshua, Saul and David. Unfortunately only
nineteen scenes survive as evidence of the mid-twelfth-century
version of the cycle, comprising of twelve scenes of the life of
Moses, one of Joshua, one of Saul, and five of David. If the circa
1200 Great Canterbury Psalter is a copy of this or a similar
series of pictures, the leaf beginning with the Moses scenes
presumably was preceded with a leaf containing at least
twenty-four scenes of Genesis. The loss of this leaf from the
mid-twelfth-century series is extremely regrettable, for the
choice of Genesis scenes might throw further light on the
choices in the thirteenth-century manuscripts. As the manuscript assuredly antedates any of the paraphrases produced
later in the century, the reasons for its choice of scenes must be
sought elsewhere, perhaps from the tradition of frontispieces to
the books of the Bible which dates back to Carolingian times, or
perhaps from contemporary works of exegesis. The Moses,
Joshua, Saul and David scenes seem insufficient in number to
enable any analysis of this problem, which must be left unre-
solved. Although the circa 1200 copy has been included for
comparison with the thirteenth-century cycles, its choice of
scenes must involve a consideration of the earlier version or
versions, and that cannot be done within the limited scope of
this paper. The listing of scenes in the Appendix reveals that the
Great Canterbury Psalter is not as closely related to the
thirteenth-century cycles as they are to each other. A number of
scenes can be seen to be unique to the Canterbury Psalter.[26]
The conclusion that could be drawn is that, unlike them, it is
very little influenced by the new texts of biblical paraphrases,
but depends rather on an earlier tradition, which could be either
pictorial or textual.

Almost contemporary with the Great Canterbury Psalter is
that in the University Library of Leiden, perhaps made for
Geoffrey Plantagenet, archbishop of York, around 1200, proba-

---

[26] Noah leaving the Ark, Joseph filling the storehouses of Pharaoh
with corn, Pharaoh ordering the midwives to kill all the male children,
the birth of Moses, the carrying of the Ark, David offered armor by
Saul, and David bringing the head of Goliath to Saul.

bly at some center in the North of England.[27] It has twenty-six scenes of the Creation, and the lives of Adam and Eve, Cain and Abel, Noah, Abraham, Joseph, and Samson.

Also around 1200, or perhaps of the first decade of the century, is the Munich Psalter, probably made in Oxford for a patron who had some connection with Gloucester, and who may have been a woman.[28] This is by far the most extensively illustrated of all the Psalters, with 176 scenes of the Creation, and of the lives of Adam and Eve, Cain and Abel, Noah, Abraham and Lot, Isaac, Jacob and Joseph, Moses, Joshua, Ruth, Samuel, David, Daniel, Susanna, Holofernes, Judith, Esther, and Jonah, with some additional scenes of other figures (figs. 7, 8).

Perhaps also from Oxford, circa 1220, is the Huntingfield Psalter in the Pierpont Morgan Library.[29] The lack of both calendar and litany make it difficult to be certain either of its provenance or patron. There are forty-five Old Testament scenes of the Creation, Adam and Eve, Cain and Abel, Noah, Abraham and Lot, Isaac, Jacob and Joseph, Moses, Joshua, Jephthah, Samuel, and David.

From a period shortly after the Huntingfield Psalter, probably circa 1220–1230, is a fragmentary cycle of twenty-four scenes in the Psalter, Cambridge, Trinity College MS. B.11.4. The manuscript was probably produced in London, perhaps for a Winchester patron who was an abbess or prioress of either a Benedictine or Augustinian nunnery.[30] The different forms of representation of the habit of this lady make the identification

---

[27] See H. Omont, *Miniatures du Psautier de St. Louis* (Leyden, 1902), for a facsimile, and Morgan, *Early Gothic Manuscripts 1190–1250*, no. 14, for a discussion of place of origin and ownership.

[28] See H. B. Graham, "Old Testament Cycles in the English Psalter in Munich" (Ph.D. diss., Princeton University, 1975); H. B. Graham, "The Munich Psalter," in *The Year 1200: A Symposium, New York, Metropolitan Museum of Art*, ed. J. Hoffeld (New York, 1975), 301–12; Morgan, *Early Gothic Manuscripts 1190–1250*, no. 23, for a description of the iconography.

[29] See Morgan, *Early Gothic Manuscripts 1190–1250*, no. 30, for a description and discussion of dating and place of production.

[30] See Morgan, *Early Gothic Manuscripts 1190–1250*, no. 51, for discussion of place of origin and ownership.

of her religious order uncertain. Regrettably, the page depicting the scenes from the Creation to Noah is lacking, and there may also have been lost scenes from Exodus and subsequent books after the end of the Joseph sequence. That which remains illustrates the lives of Abraham, Lot, Isaac, Jacob and Joseph. The scenes are arranged in a grid six to a page, a reduced version of the format of the Great Canterbury Psalter (figs. 11–13).

In the 1230s or 1240s the Oxford workshop of William de Brailes produced the set of Bible pictures which Hanns Swarzenski had discovered in Baltimore, and which had led him to the discussion of English thirteenth-century Old Testament cycles in his article of 1938. The leaves are now all as singletons, some not in the correct order, and were probably bound together and given a binding decorated with an ivory by the Paris dealer Gruel late in the nineteenth century.[31] Further leaves were discovered by Eric Millar in the Wildenstein Collection, and these are now in the Musée Marmottan in Paris.[32] Almost certainly the original manuscript contained other leaves, now either lost or in private hands, but it is difficult to reconstruct what is missing. Only an examination of the singleton leaves in the Baltimore manuscript in an unbound state might enable some reconstruction of the original bifolio arrangement. Comparison with the selective nature of subject matter in the other Psalters would suggest that the de Brailes manuscript also contained, not a continuous narrative cycle, but a selection of stories appropriate for its patron, and perhaps stipulated in its commission. Altogether thirty-six Old Testament scenes survive: the Creation, Fall of the Rebel Angels, lives of Adam and Eve, Noah, Abraham, Lot, Jacob and Joseph, Moses, Joshua, Ruth, and Samuel (figs. 5, 6, 9, 10). Each miniature has a *titulus* in French.

The final example is the Psalter in St. John's College Cam-

---

[31] See Morgan, *Early Gothic Manuscripts 1190–1250*, no. 71.

[32] E. G. Millar, "Additional Miniatures by W. De Brailes," *Journal of the Walters Art Gallery* 2 (1939): 106–9, and Morgan, *Early Gothic Manuscripts 1190–1250*, no. 71.

bridge MS. K.26 of circa 1270–1280.[33] The original Psalter text has been replaced by one of the late fourteenth century, but as the last of the thirteenth-century miniatures shows David, author of the Psalms, harping, it is clear that the pictures preceded a Psalter. There are sixteen Old Testament scenes of the Creation, and lives of Adam and Eve, Cain and Abel, Noah, Abraham, and one of Solomon (fig. 4). The lack of the original text makes it impossible to determine patron or place of production.

The choice and distribution of scenes in these ten English cycles is extremely variable both in the stories told and the number of scenes allotted to each character. Some of the episodes illustrated are unusual, whereas other famous events in some of the cycles are omitted. The selection of scenes and the way they are represented raise the issues of the interrelationship of visual and textual models. It also is a leading question as to whether the artists were allowed free interpretation within the general framework of a commission, or whether they were precisely instructed by intermediaries acting on behalf of their patrons. It is reasonable to assume that in almost all these works of art such intermediaries, educated clerics, were necessary for communicating the wishes of a patron to the artists. Or, if the patron had no specific wishes, such men could have planned out an appropriate program of Bible history as they thought fit. The influence from the biblical paraphrases very probably results from the clerical advisor rather than any direct knowledge of the texts by the artists themselves.

Certain stories, in particular those of Joseph, Moses, and David, range in number of scenes from one or two to over twenty.[34] Some characters, notably Isaac, or Jacob in the early

[33] G. D. S. Henderson, "MS K.26 in the Library of St. John's College, Cambridge. A Study of the Style and Iconography of its Thirteenth Century Illustrations" (Ph.D. diss., Cambridge University, 1959); Morgan, *Early Gothic Manuscripts 1250–1285*, no. 179, for discussion and full bibliography. See G. D. S. Henderson, "Studies in English Manuscript Illumination: Part III: The English Apocalypse, II," *Journal of the Warburg and Courtauld Institutes* 31 (1968): 145–47, for an alternative view of dating.

[34] The life of Joseph seems to have been a subject favored by Henry

part of his life, are given surprisingly brief coverage.[35] Scenes of Enoch, Balaam, Jephthah, Daniel, Susanna, Samson, Solomon, Holofernes, Judith, Esther, and Jonah, only occur in one out of the ten cycles. Even the Munich Psalter with its extensive series of most of these stories surprisingly completely lacks pictures of the lives of such famous figures as Samson and Solomon.

It seems highly likely that the patron or his advisor selected a number of stories for the artists to illustrate which were appropriate as a didactic program, or which had personal significance for the patron.[36] If the advisor was a chaplain or confessor of the patron, the main motivation may have been for religious instruction. If the patron was directly involved in stipulating the details of the commission, then the personal significance of the scenes chosen may predominate as the principle for their selection. Each cycle is different in emphasis because it reflects a different patronage situation, a different sort of advisor to the artists, or a different relationship between the advisor and the artists.

Regrettably, in only two cases in the manuscripts is there evidence of a patron: the Great Canterbury Psalter made for the Benedictines of Christ Church, Canterbury, and the Leiden Psalter made probably, but not absolutely certainly, for Geoffrey

---

III, as evidenced by wall paintings under the king's patronage: T. Borenius, "The Cycle of Images in the Palaces and Castles of Henry III," *Journal of the Warburg and Courtauld Institutes* 4 (1943): 43, 49; E. W. Tristram, *English Medieval Wall Painting: The Thirteenth Century* (Oxford, 1950), 477. In no way connected with English art but for an interesting parallel of a thirteenth-century Joseph cycle under royal patronage see: R. Ljubinković, "Sur le symbolisme de l'histoire de Joseph du narthex de Sopoćani," *L'Art Byzantin du XIIIe siècle. Symposium de Sopoćani, 1965*, ed. V. J. Djurić (Belgrade, 1967), 207–37.

[35] An exceptional example of many scenes for the early life of Jacob is the lost cycle of paintings from the choir enclosure of Bury St. Edmunds: James, *St. Edmund at Bury*, 201.

[36] An interesting study of an Old Testament cycle prefacing a Psalter relating the choice of scenes to the patron is: W.C. Jordan, "The Psalter of Saint Louis (BN MS. lat. 10525): The Program of the Seventy-Eight Full-Page Illustrations," in *The High Middle Ages*, ed. Penelope C. Mayo, ACTA, vol. 7 (Binghamton, 1983), 65–91.

Plantagenet, archbishop of York.[37] The particular problem of the cycle of the Canterbury Psalter as a possible copy of a mid-twelfth-century model has been discussed earlier. The Leiden Psalter is unusual both in its choice of Abraham scenes and in the series of Samson scenes of which it is unique among all the cycles.

The Munich Psalter emphasizes the lives of heroic women, Ruth, Susanna, Judith, and Esther. Although Ruth scenes occur in the de Brailes manuscript, the other lives are unique to the Munich Psalter. The examples of the virtues of these women would most likely be appropriate for a female patron. Such hypotheses concerning the type of patron could perhaps be made for the other cycles, but in none of them is there such an obvious indication of emphasis on certain stories such as the lives of women in the Munich Psalter. It may be possible with further study to define the character of a cycle such that it could be seen as appropriate to a particular class of patron, clerical or lay, for the monastic or secular church, for men or for women, or even for children.

For the cycles in monumental art the patronage is of course known in general terms, but the individuals who supervised the commission are not. At Sigena the convent was a royal foundation for nuns of the order of St. John of Jerusalem, and Wells and Salisbury were secular cathedrals. At Salisbury, as at Sigena, the Old Testament cycle decorates a Chapter House. The dating of all of these three monuments is controversial, and the precise date is of course relevant if the Old Testament scenes are to be associated with the interests of a particular patron, or with the issues of a particular moment in time.

If the choice of the stories to be represented were a result of the patronage there is still the further problem of the exact choice of scenes within these stories. It is in this aspect that the importance of the biblical paraphrases becomes clear. In the choice of scenes in the life of a particular figure the interests of

---

[37] See Morgan, *Early Gothic Manuscripts 1190–1250*, no. 14, for a discussion of the place of production and ownership.

the patron may be very strong, but the paraphrases influenced this choice and the way the story was told. The evidence of this influence is above all to be found in the extra-biblical elements, and in the preference for rare episodes which were extracted by Petrus Comestor, Peter of Riga, or Peter of Poitiers in the *Historia scholastica*, the *Aurora*, and the *Compendium*. The vernacular paraphrases such as the "Bible" of Herman of Valenciennes, the Middle English Genesis and Exodus, and *Iacob and Iosep*, and *Cursor Mundi*, depend heavily on these three Latin works which were essential as the basic reference books on biblical history and exegesis.[38] The *Historia scholastica* and the *Aurora* were, towards the end of the thirteenth century, to be translated into vernacular versions in France by Guyart Desmoulins and Macé de la Charité, and were used as a source by other translators of the Bible into French.[39] Guyart Desmou-

---

[38] Of the references in n. 10 the following studies give information on the links with Peter Comestor and Peter of Riga: P. E. Beichner, "The Cursor Mundi and Petrus Riga," *Speculum* 24 (1949): 239–50; A. Fritzsche, "Ist die altenglische 'Story of Genesis and Exodus' das Werk eines Verfassers?" *Anglia* 5 (1882): 43–90; Spiele, *Li Romanz*, 25–36. The abbreviated accounts of Old Testament history at the beginning of Universal Chronicles also depend on these three sources: see T. Jones, "The *Promptuarium Bibliae* as a source of Roger of Wendover's *Flores Historiarum* and of Ranulph Higden's *Polychronicon*," *Aberystwyth Studies* 14 (1936): 53–67.

[39] The translations of Guyart Desmoulins and Macé de la Charité should be set beside other French versions of the biblical text which probably were also influential on artists in France, and perhaps also in England. On French translations in general see S. Berger, *La Bible Française au Moyen Age* (Paris, 1884); J. Bonnard, *Les traductions de la Bible en vers français au Moyen Age* (Paris, 1884); F. Bonnardot, "Fragments d'une traduction de la Bible en vers français," *Romania* 16 (1887): 177–213; P. Meyer, Review of Berger, *Bible Française* and Bonnard, *Traductions de la Bible, Romania* 17 (1888): 121–44; E. R. Curtius, *Li Quatre Livre des Reis* (Dresden, 1911); M. D. Legge, *Anglo-Norman Literature and Its Background* (Oxford, 1963), 176–80; G. de Poerck and R. van Deyck, "La Bible et l'activité traductrice dans les pays romans avant 1300," in H. R. Jauss, *La littérature didactique, allégorique et satirique. Grundriss der romanischen Literaturen des Mittelalters*, 6 (Heidelberg, 1968), vol.1, 21–47; vol. 2, 54–80; J. R. Smeets, "Les traductions, adaptations et paraphrases de la Bible en vers," in Jauss, *La Littérature didactique, allégorique et satirique*, vol. 1, 48–57; vol. 2, 81–96; C. R. Sneddon, "The 'Bible du XIIIe siècle':

lins's version of the *Historia scholastica* as the *Bible historiale*
becomes extensively illustrated in France in the fourteenth and
fifteenth centuries, but no examples survive which were produced in England.[40]

The influence of the paraphrases is first evident in the increase of apocryphal elements in the pictorial narrative. Such
extra-biblical material had of course been known in some cases
long before the thirteenth century, but not much had penetrated
into art or had been available in a compilation as comprehen-
sive as the *Historia scholastica*. Josephus, in the *Antiquitates
Iudaicae*, had been a source for the introduction of Jewish legendary material as a supplement to the account of the Vulgate.
Biblical commentators had introduced piece by piece apocryphal

---

Its Medieval Public in the Light of Its Manuscript Tradition," in *The
Bible and Medieval Culture*, ed. W. Lourdaux and D. Verhelst, Mediae-
valia Lovanensia, 7 (Leuven, 1979), 127–40; J. Leclercq, "Les traductions
de la Bible et la spiritualité médiévale," in *The Bible and Medieval Culture*,
263–77; J. R. Smeets, "Les traductions-adaptations versifiées de la Bible
en ancien français" and P. M. Bogaert, "Adaptations et versions de la
Bible en prose(langue d'oil)," both in *Les genres littéraires dans les sources
théologiques et philosophiques mediévales, Actes du Colloque International de
Louvain-la-Neuve (1981)* (Louvain, 1982), 249–58 and 259–78; D. A.
Trotter, "The Influence of Bible Commentaries on Old French Bible
Translations," *Medium Aevum* 56 (1987): 257–75. On the Bible of Macé de
la Charité: P. E. Beichner, "The Old French Bible of Macé de la Charité,
a Translation of the Aurora," *Speculum* 22 (1947): 226–39; J. R. Smeets, P.
E. R. Verhuyck, A. M. L. Prangsma-Hajenius, H. C. M. van der Krabben,
La Bible de Macé de la Charité, 1–4 (Leiden, 1964–77). On the Bible of
Jehan Malkaraume: P. E. Beichner, "La Bible versifiée de Jehan Malka-
raume et l'Aurora," *Le Moyen Age* 61 (1955): 63–78; J. R. Smeets, *La Bible
de Jehan Malkaraume* (Assen, 1978); J. R. Smeets, "La Bible de Jehan
Malkaraume," in *The Bible and Medieval Culture*, 127–40. On the Bible des
Septs Etats du Monde: P. Meyer, "Notice sur la Bible des Septs Etats du
Monde de Geufroi de Paris," *Notices et Extraits des Manuscrits de la
Bibliothèque Nationale* 39, part 1 (1909): 255–322; J. R. Smeets, "Les
Sources de Geufroi de Paris," *Rapports het franse boek* 51 (1981): 97–109.
On Guyart Desmoulins, *Bible historiale* see Berger, *La Bible Francaise*, 157–
87. For the text of the *Bible historiale* there is only the 1537–38 two
volume edition printed in Paris: *La Bible en françois*.

[40] For some French examples see M. Meiss, *French Painting in the
Time of Jean de Berry: The Boucicaut Master* (London, 1968), 96–99; *French
Painting in the Time of Jean de Berry: The Limbourgs and their Contemporar-
ies* (London, 1974), 339–42.

detail, and the achievement of Petrus Comestor was to draw this diverse material together.[41] Not all elements of the extra-biblical accounts in the vernacular paraphrases occur in the *Historia scholastica*, and although scholars have been defining sources for these works for over a century, some are still not clear. A few examples will now be cited of the use of this apocryphal material in the English Old Testament cycles.[42]

Discussion of the iconography of each scene in relation to these textual sources cannot be attempted in this brief study, and the examples of some scenes from the lives of Adam and Eve, Cain, and Joseph will demonstrate my general thesis concerning the importance of the paraphrases both in their Latin and vernacular versions. In many cases the strict biblical account without elaboration is adhered to both in the illustrations and in the paraphrases themselves. In such cases it would be almost impossible to assess whether the artists knew the iconography from established visual traditions, from knowledge of the Vulgate text, or from the version of the Vulgate account in the paraphrases.

Several of the cycles show the scene of an angel assisting, or present, when Adam and Eve begin their labors on earth after their expulsion from Paradise. The Vulgate makes no mention of this instruction of Adam and Eve by the angel, and the source may be the Latin *Vita Adae et Evae*, which was adapted as a version in Middle English.[43] At Sigena and in the Leiden

---

[41] On the sources of Petrus Comestor see S. R. Karp, "Peter Comestor's 'Historia Scholastica': A Study in the Development of Literal Scriptural Exegesis" (Ph.D. diss., Tulane University, 1978).

[42] Important work has been done already on the iconography of individual scenes in relation to literature and apocryphal elements: P. F. Braude, "Cokkel in oure Clene Corn: Some Implications of Cain's Sacrifice," *Gesta* 7 (1968): 15–28; P. Z. Blum, "The Middle English Romance" cited in n. 22; R. Mellinkoff, *The Horned Moses in Medieval Art and Thought* (London, 1970); R. Mellinkoff, "Cain and the Jews," *Journal of Jewish Art* 6 (1979): 16–38; R. Mellinkoff, *The Mark of Cain* (Berkeley, 1981); R. Mellinkoff, "More about Horned Moses," *Journal of Jewish Art* 12/13 (1986/87): 184–98.

[43] A. C. Dunstan, "The Middle English *Canticum de Creatione* and the Latin *Vita Adae et Evae*," *Anglia* 55 (1931): 431–42. For the Latin text: W. Meyer, *Vita Adae et Evae*, *Abhandlungen der philosophisch-philologischen Classe der Königlich Bayerischen Akademie der Wissenschaften* 14 (1878), 228;

Psalter the angel is shown instructing Adam to dig. In the short cycle in the Carrow Psalter the angel flies down with the spade for Adam and the spindle for Eve (fig. 3).[44] In the St. John's Psalter the angel flies down to assist or speak to Adam and Eve while they are at their labors (fig. 4). Even though there may be pictorial precedents for these motifs in the twelfth century or earlier, these scenes are in the same spirit as the passage in the Middle English Genesis and Exodus in which the angel comes to them in their distress after their expulsion. They are comforted in their sadness by being told that one day the Son of God will again bring man to Paradise.[45] They are not abandoned by God, for he sends his angel to help them.

Of much older origin, but taken up in the *Historia scholastica* and the Middle English Genesis and Exodus, is the story of Lamech's blindness.[46] The Vulgate text is vague concerning the exact description of the event in which Lamech shoots Cain with an arrow, and merely narrates that Lamech had slain a man (Gen. 4.23). The story in the paraphrases tells how Lamech, who is almost blind, is led about by a boy and that he shot Cain with an arrow. In the Munich and Huntingfield Psalters this incident is illustrated, and also in the sculpture of Wells. In the Old Testament scenes on a single leaf from the de Brailes workshop now in the Fitzwilliam Museum, Cambridge, MS. 330 the scene is shown without the boy (fig. 2).[47]

J. H. Mozley, "The 'Vita Adae,'" *Journal of Theological Studies* 30 (1929): 134.

[44] The angel stands giving the spade and spindle in the c. 1150 Winchester Psalter and in the sculpture of c. 1170–80 of the South Porch at Malmesbury: Haney, *Winchester Psalter*, 76–77. The angel instructing occurs first in English art in Aelfric's Hexateuch.

[45] Morris, *Genesis and Exodus*, lines 397–408.

[46] *Historia scholastica*, col. 1079; *Genesis and Exodus*, lines 471–81. For this episode see H. Dürrschmidt, *Die Sage von Kain in der mittelalterlichen Literatur Englands* (Bayreuth, 1919), 47, 89. A textual source of an early date would be the Revelations of the pseudo-Methodius: E. Sackur, *Sibyllinische Texte und Forschungen* (Halle, 1898), 62; C. d'Evelyn, "The Middle English Metrical Version of the Revelations of Methodius with a Study of the Influence of Methodius on Middle English Writings," *Publications of the Modern Language Association* 33 (1918): 154, 160.

[47] For a discussion of the leaves, see Morgan, *Early Gothic Manuscripts 1190–1250*, no. 72.

The story of Jacob and Joseph was interpolated with apocryphal elements both in the paraphrases and in the pictures.[48]
Pamela Blum has clearly demonstrated that the sculpture cycle
at Salisbury was closely dependent on the Middle English poem
Iacob and Iosep, written in the second quarter of the thirteenth
century.[49] The poet takes elements from both the *Historia scholastica* and the "Bible" of Herman of Valenciennes.[50] The best
example would be the incident of Joseph rejecting the advances
of Potiphar's wife (fig. 8). The variant of the Joseph story is that
the Ishmaelites sold Joseph not to Potiphar but to Pharaoh, and
as an apocryphal story it goes back to Early Christian times.[51]
It is therefore the queen of Egypt who attempts to seduce him
(fig. 14). In the Trinity Psalter he is shown sold to a crowned
man who is intended as Pharaoh (fig. 11) The inscription in the
de Brailes Psalter in the scene of the woman complaining
against Joseph identifies her as "la femme (de) pharaon," and
this picture parallels the dramatic complaint of the queen which
is found in the paraphrases (fig. 9).[52] The apocryphal version
of the story is not always followed. The Munich Psalter shows
Joseph sold to Potiphar, and the woman is not crowned (fig. 8).

At Salisbury there is the scene of Joseph taken to the prison
in which the butler and baker are already in their cell. The same
apocryphal variant is found in Herman of Valenciennes.[53] The

---

[48] See nn. 50, 51 for references.

[49] See n. 22. For illustrations see S. Whittingham, *Salisbury Chapter House* (Salisbury, 1979).

[50] For the legends of Joseph in literature see F. E. Faverty, "Legends of Joseph in Old and Middle English," *Publications of the Modern Language Association* 43 (1928): 79–104. A thirteenth-century French story of Joseph with relatively little non-biblical elements is edited by E. Sass, *L'Estoire Joseph* (Dresden, 1906). For the exegesis of the Joseph story by medieval commentators see M. Derpmann, *Die Josephsgeschichte* (Düsseldorf, 1974).

[51] F. E. Faverty, "The Story of Joseph and Potiphar's Wife in Mediaeval Literature," *Harvard Studies and Notes in Philology and Literature* 13 (1931): 81–127; J. R. Smeets, "Le monologue de la Roïne dans la Bible de Malkaraume," *Mélanges Lein Geschiere* (Amsterdam, 1975), 11–24.

[52] See the article by Smeets cited in n. 51.

[53] Spiele, *Li Romanz*, lines 1318–24.

Bible has it the other way around, with Joseph put in prison first. Another legendary Joseph scene found at Salisbury is the throwing of chaff on the Nile. The Israelites who see this chaff floating on the river conclude that there is corn in Egypt, and go down to Egypt to purchase it. The "Bible" of Herman of Valenciennes has this incident, and it is narrated in the late thirteenth-century *Cursor Mundi*.[54]

Outside of the narrative cycles works of art show the influence of the expanded biblical narrative of the paraphrases. The Oscott Psalter of circa 1265–1270 has the scene of God carrying Adam to Paradise, the episode referred to briefly in the Vulgate in Gen. 2.15, but singled out for extended treatment in some of the paraphrases.[55] The Bible of William of Hales, a Salisbury product of 1254, has for its Exodus initial the apocryphal incident of the child Moses throwing down the crown which Pharaoh had given him.[56] The incident is described in Josephus and is followed in the *Historia scholastica*.[57]

Not only in the representation of apocryphal incidents is there evidence of the influence of the paraphrases, but also in the choice of scenes and their order which sometimes differs from the narrative order of the Bible.[58] The clearest example is the Munich Psalter, many of whose unusual subjects are found in the *Aurora* of Peter of Riga.[59] The exceptionally rare scenes

[54] Spiele, *Li Romanz*, lines 1541–78; Napier, *Iacob and Iosep*, xii–xiii; Morris, *Cursor Mundi*, lines 4749–92. For the Salisbury scenes see Blum, "The Middle English Romance," 23, 25.

[55] For example, *Genesis and Exodus*, lines 208–12. See Morgan, *Early Gothic Manuscripts 1250–1285*, no. 151, for the Oscott Psalter.

[56] Mellinkoff, "More about Horned Moses," 195, fig. 22.

[57] Flavius Josephus, *The Jewish Antiquities*, trans. H. St. J. Thackeray and R. Marcus (Cambridge, MA, 1961), book 2, 267; *Historia scholastica*, col. 1144.

[58] The choice of scenes may also be influenced by the choice of Old Testament readings in the Breviary. As so few English medieval Breviaries are edited, and also as yet no study has been made of the variants in their biblical readings, it is not at present possible to be at all certain about the extent of this influence. The majority of the Old Testament illustrations discussed in this article antedate the introduction of the use of Sarum. The Old Testament readings in the Sarum Breviary show no obvious connections with any of the cycles.

[59] It is probable that the *Aurora* was the major influence on the

of Phineas slaying Zimri and Cozbi, of David's ambassador's shaved by the Ammonites, and of David's numbering of the people, illustrating chapter 24 of 2 Kings, are singled out by Peter of Riga, who is much more selective than Petrus Comestor in his choice of material.[60] Many of the events described in the *Aurora* are found in the English Old Testament cycles, and it must be assumed that it was being used with the *Historia scholastica* as a major source for the choice of episode. The de Brailes cycle is exceptional in illustrating the plagues of Egypt (fig. 5), and this may reflect the exceedingly lengthy discussion in the *Historia scholastica*, which devotes a chapter to each plague.[61] The de Brailes manuscript and the Munich Psalter both have the odd scene in the book of Ruth of Boaz making a pact with his kinsmen by taking off his shoe (Ruth 4.7–8) (fig. 6). This episode is in the *Historia scholastica* and the *Aurora*.[62] It is very likely that the chapter and section headings in the *Historia scholastica* and *Aurora* could be influential in determining choice of subject.

A final example is that of the order of scenes in the episode of Joseph's brothers charged with the theft of the cup. In the Bible this scene occurs during the second visit of the brothers to Egypt when they have Benjamin with them, and the cup is found in Benjamin's sack (figs. 12, 13) The "Bible" of Herman of Valenciennes and *Iacob and Iosep* have the incident during the first visit to Egypt before they return to Jacob to persuade him to let them take Benjamin with them to Egypt.[63] In the Trinity Psalter the event with the cup is represented in sequence before the scene of the brothers requesting Jacob to let them take Benjamin to Egypt (figs. 12, 13). The scene is adapted from the correct biblical order scene of the money put in the brother's sacks in the picture in the Munich Psalter on which the Trinity

---

choice of scenes in the Munich Psalter. I hope to discuss this theory in more detail in a future article.

[60] Beichner (1965), Numbers, line 535; 2 Kings, lines 139–44, 347–90.

[61] *Historia scholastica*, cols. 1149–52.

[62] *Historia scholastica*, col. 1294; Beichner (1965), Ruth, lines 40–41.

[63] Spiele, *Li Romanz*, lines 1598–1646; Napier, *Iacob and Iosep*, lines 400–422.

Psalter version is directly modelled. Such changes of order of scene prove without doubt that the artists or their advisors knew of the paraphrases.

In using the paraphrases it is likely that the Latin texts of Petrus Comestor, Peter of Riga, and Peter of Poitiers were used, as well as the vernacular texts in Middle English and Anglo-Norman, for planning these cycles of pictures. It is certain that artists must also have used visual models, but these seem to have been overrated in importance in the art historical literature, and have been almost the sole aspect of previous discussion of the cycles. The theory favored is that early in the Middle Ages large cycles were created whose derivants constantly were used as source material by artists.[64] Examples of such cycles would be those of the Cotton Genesis, the Byzantine Octateuchs, and that of Aelfric's Hexateuch.[65] It has already been questioned whether the illustrations of the Anglo-Saxon paraphrases were dependent on these hypothetical early cycles, or whether the artists were mainly influenced by their paraphrase text.[66] The conclusion to be drawn from the thirteenth-century cycles is that their choice and selection of subject matter in many cases is more closely paralleled in the emphases of the paraphrases than that in the Vulgate itself, and that these texts, and individual preferences of the patron or clerical advisor, were the determining element of the content of the pictorial cycle. This does not absolutely preclude that large ancient pictorial cycles were consulted if they existed close at hand. It is, however, with some scepticism that I view this dependence on old pictorial models as a factor of much importance for the cycles of scenes in thirteenth-century English art. If there had been old pictorial cycles in the twelfth century, by the early

---

[64] These ideas have been proposed for the English thirteenth-century cycles in particular by Swarzenski, "Unknown Bible Pictures," and Henderson, "Late Antique Influences" cited in n. 3.

[65] For a study of the influence of the Cotton Genesis cycle see the excellent recent monograph by Kurt Weitzmann and Herbert Kessler cited in n. 3.

[66] In particular by Dodwell in Dodwell and Clemoes, *The Old English Illustrated Hexateuch*, 65–73, cited in n. 2.

years of the thirteenth century they had been fundamentally transformed under the influence of the paraphrase texts. The narrative character of story-telling also changes to present the Bible stories more in terms of a "romance" in which kings, queens, seneschals, younger sons, familial relationships and feudal obligations reflect themes of contemporary relevance. The early fourteenth-century Old Testament cycle in the Queen Mary Psalter (London, British Library MS. Royal 2.B.VII) would be a developed example of such "romance" presentation.[67] In that manuscript, contemporary words to describe social status are interpolated or substituted into descriptions from the Bible text used as titles to the pictures. This change also involves an adaptation of pictorial narrative in terms of the syntax of pose, gesture, and figure interrelationships, an approach to the study of iconography as yet hardly explored by art historians.

These "new" thirteenth-century cycles were certainly copied by artists for other works of art. There are several close correspondences in composition of scenes between the Munich Psalter and the Trinity Psalter suggesting that the Trinity manuscript must directly derive from the Munich Psalter or its model. As I discussed previously, there are in the Trinity manuscript several significant changes derived from texts, such as the substitute of the cup for the purse of money in the scene of the sacks of Joseph's brothers. Between the various works there is in most cases notable differences in composition of a particular scene, and it might be suggested that often the artists had no pictorial model but only knowledge of a text.

The popular occurrence of these Old Testament scenes in Psalters suggests that they fulfilled in many cases a didactic function. The Psalter was the book used as a primer for the learning of Latin with the Psalms as the texts to be construed.[68] The pictures would have served as narrative stories

---

[67] G. F. Warner, *Queen Mary's Psalter* (London, 1912). Another fourteenth-century example of such vernacularization of pictorial narrative would be the Holkham Bible picture book: W. O. Hassall, *The Holkham Bible Picture Book* (London, 1954).

[68] The suggestion that this was a function of the illustrated versions was made long ago by L. Delisle, "Livres d'images destinés à l'instruc-

for children, as moral exemplars for the laity, and could be given an exegetical interpretation by the better educated. The Leiden Psalter later belonged to St. Louis of France, and a later hand has written a description of its educational function at the foot of the page of the initial of the first psalm: "Cist psautiers fuit mon seigneur saint loys qui fu roys de france: ou quel il apprist en s'enfance."[69] Both the text and pictures served a didactic function, and the pictures could have been supplemented by further reading in the vernacular biblical paraphrases, which increase in number as the thirteenth century progresses. Although the text of the Vulgate was readily available with the increase in production of the small portable Bible, most members of the laity probably received their knowledge of the stories of the Old Testament in texts or pictures incorporating elements from legendary material and contemporary literary expansions of the narrative in a "romance" form available in the vernacular. As literacy increased so did the market for such vernacular literature, and by the fourteenth century apocryphal biblical texts full of anecdotal incident must have been much more familiar than the text of the Bible itself.[70] To many people the stories of the Old Testament were familiar, but both in

---

tion des laïques," *Histoire Littéraire de la France* 31 (1893): 213–85. For the very old tradition of the Psalter as a textbook see: P. Riché, "Le psautier, livre de lecture élémentaire," in *Etudes mérovingiennes* (Paris, 1953), 253–56. A good description of elementary education in thirteenth-century France involving the use of the Psalter is given in P. Dubois, *The Recovery of the Holy Land*, trans. W. I. Brandt (New York, 1956), 126. The Psalter would be replaced in the later thirteenth century by the Book of Hours as a primer. This prayer book was called by the name of primer in later medieval England. A good account of its use in elementary education as well as that of the Psalter is given in N. Orme, *English Schools in the Middle Ages* (London, 1973), 62.

[69] For a color plate of this page see *Le siècle de Saint Louis*, ed. R. Pernoud (Paris, 1970), opposite p. 112.

[70] For general studies on the rise of literacy see M. B. Parkes, "The Literacy of the Laity," in *Literature and Western Civilization: The Medieval Period*, ed. D. Daiches and A. K. Thorlby (London, 1973), 555–77; M. T. Clanchy, *From Memory to Written Record* (Cambridge, MA, 1979), 175–201; F. H. Bäuml, "Varieties and Consequences of Medieval Literacy and Illiteracy," *Speculum* 55 (1980): 237–65.

pictures and texts they had been adapted in ways such that they resembled more the romances of contemporary writers, and thus presented narrative contexts appropriate to the tastes and issues of the time.

Appendix

Old Testament Narrative Scenes in English Thirteenth-Century Art

Sigla :

MSS:	Paris Bibliothèque Nationale lat. 8846	Ca
	Leiden, Bibl. Rijksuniversiteit lat. 76A	Ld
	Munich, Bayerisches Staatsbibl.Clm. 835	Mu
	New York, Pierpont Morgan Lib. M. 43	Hu
	Cambridge, Trinity Coll. B.11.4	Tr
	Baltimore, Walters Art Gall. W.106	Br
	Paris, Musée Marmottan,Coll.Wildenstein	Br
	Cambridge, St. John's Coll. K.26	Jo
Painting:		
	Sigena, Chapter House	Sg
Sculpture:		
	Wells, Cathedral, West Front	We
	Salisbury, Cathedral, Chapter House	Sa

Biblical references are to the Douay-Rheims version of the Bible.

Creation and Fall of the Angels
Creation Scenes: Ca, Ld, Mu, Hu, Br, Jo, Sg, We, Sa
Text: Gen. 1.1–27
Fall of the Rebel Angels: Br
Text: Apocryphal

Adam and Eve
Adam and Eve: instructed by God: Ca, Ld, Mu, Sg, We, Sa
Text: Gen. 2.16,17
Adam and Eve: tempted by the Serpent: Ca, Ld, Mu, Hu, Jo, Sg, We, Sa

Text: Gen. 3.1–6
Adam and Eve: reprimanded by God: Ld, Mu, We, Sa
Text: Gen. 3.8–13
Adam and Eve: clothed by God: Br
Text: Gen. 3.21
Adam and Eve: expulsion from Paradise: Ca, Ld, Mu, Hu, Br,
   Jo, Sg, We, Sa
Text: Gen. 3.24
Adam: instructed to dig by the Angel: Ld, Jo, Sg
Text: Apocryphal
Adam: digging: Ca, Ld, Mu, Jo, Sg, We, Sa
Text: Gen. 3.23
Eve: instructed to spin by the Angel: Ld, Jo
Text: Apocryphal
Eve: spinning: Ca, Ld, Mu, Jo, Sg, We, Sa
Text: Apocryphal

Cain and Abel
Cain and Abel: make their offerings: Ca, Ld, Mu, Hu, Jo, Sg,
   We, Sa
Text: Gen. 4.3–5
Cain: murders Abel: Ca, Ld, Mu, Hu, Jo, Sg, Sa
Text: Gen. 4.8
Cain: rebuked by God: Ca, Mu, Hu, Jo, Sa
Text: Gen. 4.9–12
Cain: shot by Lamech: Mu, Hu, We
Text: Gen. 4.23 and Apocryphal

Enoch
Enoch: ascension: Mu
Text: Gen. 5.24

Noah
Noah: instructed to build the ark: Ld, Mu, Jo, Sa
Text: Gen. 6.14–22
Noah: building the ark: Ld, Mu, Hu, Jo, Sg, We, Sa
Text: Gen. 6.22
Noah: entering the ark: Br, Jo, Sg, Sa
Text: Gen. 7.7–9, 13–16

Noah: in the ark: Ca, Br, Sg, We
Text: Gen. 7.23
The Flood: Br
Text: Gen. 7.17–24
Noah: receives the dove: Ld, Mu, Hu, Sg, Sa
Text: Gen. 8.8–11
Noah: leaving the ark: Ca
Text: Gen. 8.18, 19
Noah: tending vines: Ca, We(?), Sa
Text: Gen. 9.20
Noah: drunkenness: Ca, Ld, Mu, Hu, Sg, Sa
Text: Gen. 9.21–23

Tower of Babel
Building of the Tower of Babel: Mu, Hu, Sa
Text: Gen. 11.4–9

Abraham and Lot
Abraham: battle with the four kings: Mu, Hu
Text: Gen. 14.1–10
Abraham: offered bread and wine by Melchisedech: Ca, Mu,
Hu, Tr, Jo
Text: Gen. 14.18,19
Abraham: covenant with God: Ld
Text: Gen. 17.15–22
Abraham: circumcising Ishmael: Ld
Text: Gen. 17.25–26
Abraham: worships the three angels: Jo, Sa
Text: Gen. 18.2
Abraham: entertains the three angels: Ld, Mu, Hu, Tr, Br, Jo
Text: Gen. 18.1–10
Lot: barring the Sodomites: Hu, Br
Text: Gen. 19.4–11
Lot: departs from Sodom: Mu, Hu, Tr, Br, Sa
Text: Gen. 19.17–28
Abraham: journey to the sacrifice: Sa
Text: Gen. 22.3
Abraham: sacrifice of Isaac: Ca, Ld, Mu, Hu, Tr, Jo, Sg
Text: Gen. 22.13,14

Isaac
Isaac: meeting with Rebecca: Mu, Hu, Tr, We(?)
Text: Gen. 24.63–66
Isaac: blesses Jacob: Ca, Mu, Hu, Tr, We(?), Sa
Text: Gen. 27.18–29
Isaac: brought food by Esau: Mu, Hu, Tr, Sa
Text: Gen. 27.30–33

Jacob and Joseph
Jacob: sent by Rebecca to Mesopotamia of Syria: Sa
Text: Gen. 27.42–45
Jacob: his dream: Ca, Mu, Tr, Sa
Text: Gen. 28.11–15
Jacob and Rachel at well: Sa
Text: Gen. 29.9–12
Jacob: meeting with Laban: Sa
Text: Gen. 29.13
Jacob: wrestling with the angel: Ca, Mu, Hu, Tr, Sa
Text: Gen. 32.24–27
Jacob: meeting with Esau: Sa
Text: Gen. 33.3–15
Joseph: dreams of the sheaves of wheat and sun and moon: Sa
Text: Gen. 37.7–9
Joseph: tells his dream: Sa
Text: Gen. 37.10
Jacob: sends Joseph to his brothers in Shechem: Mu, Tr, Br
Text: Gen. 37.13,14
Joseph: comes to his brothers: Mu, Tr, Sa
Text: Gen. 37.23
Joseph: thrown into the pit: Ca, Sa
Text: Gen. 37.24
Joseph: sold by his brothers: Ca, Ld, Mu, Tr, Br, Sa
Text: Gen. 37.28
Joseph: his garments made bloody: Sa
Text: Gen. 37.31
Jacob: shown Joseph's garment: Sa
Text: Gen. 37.32–35
Joseph: sold to Potiphar (or Pharaoh): Mu, Tr, Sa
Text: Gen. 39.1

Joseph: flees from Potiphar's (Pharaoh's) wife: Mu, Hu, Tr, Sa
Text: Gen. 39.7–12
Joseph: accused by Potiphar's (Pharaoh's) wife: Br, Sa
Text: Gen. 39.14–19
Joseph: put in prison with Pharaoh's butler and baker: Sa
Text: Gen. 39.20
Joseph: in prison with Pharaoh's butler and baker: Mu, Hu, Tr
Text: Gen. 40.3,4
Joseph: Pharaoh served by the butler, the baker hanged: Mu, Tr, Sa
Text: Gen. 40.20–22
Pharaoh: dreams of the ears of corn and the kine: Sa
Text: Gen. 41.1–7
Pharaoh: consults wise men concerning his dream: Sa
Text: Gen. 41.8
Joseph: released from prison: Sa
Text: Gen. 41.14
Joseph: interprets Pharaoh's dream: Mu, Tr, Sa
Text: Gen. 41.14–31
Joseph: presides over threshing of corn: Sa
Text: Gen. 41.47
Joseph: filling the storehouses of Pharaoh with corn: Ca
Text: Gen. 41.49
Joseph: riding by the granaries of Egypt: Mu, Tr
Text: Gen. 41.46–49
Joseph: corn is thrown on the Nile: Sa
Text: Apocryphal
Jacob: sends his sons to buy corn in Egypt: Hu
Text: Gen. 42.1,2
Joseph: asks his brothers to return with Benjamin: Sa
Text: Gen. 42.20
Joseph: his brothers' sacks are filled with corn: Mu, Tr, Sa
Text: Gen. 42.25
Joseph: his brothers find money in their sacks: Mu
Text. Gen. 42.27–28
Jacob: persuaded to send Benjamin to Egypt: Mu, Tr
Text: Gen. 43.7–14
Joseph: Benjamin comes before him: Sa
Text: Gen. 43.29

Joseph: the cup is put in Benjamin's sack: Sa
Text: Gen. 44.1–2.
Joseph: his brothers charged with the theft of the cup: Tr, Br (in
   Tr the picture precedes Jacob: persuaded to send Benjamin to
   Egypt)
Text: Gen. 44.6–7
Joseph: Benjamin charged with the theft of the cup: Sa
Text: Gen. 44.12
Joseph: makes himself known to his brothers: Sa
Text: Gen. 45.3–15
Joseph: farewell to Benjamin: Mu, Tr, Sa
Text: Gen. 45.22
Jacob: arrives with his family in Egypt: Ca, Mu, Tr, Sa
Text: Gen. 46.5–7
Joseph: meeting with Jacob: Br, Sa
Text: Gen. 46.29
Jacob: presented to Pharaoh: Ca, Mu, Tr, Sa
Text: Gen. 47.7–10
Jacob: blesses Ephraim and Manasseh: Mu, Tr, We(?)
Text: Gen. 48.9–20
Jacob: blesses all his sons: Mu
Text: Gen. 49.1–27

Moses
Pharaoh: orders the midwives to kill all male children: Ca
Text: Exod. 1.15–22
Moses: birth: Ca
Text: Exod. 2.1–2
Moses: rescued from the Nile: Ca, Mu
Text: Exod. 2.3–9
Moses: kills the Egyptian and buries him in the sand: Mu
Text: Exod. 2.11,12
Moses: the Burning Bush: Ca, Mu, Hu, Sa
Text: Exod. 3.2
Moses: with Aaron before Pharaoh: Mu
Text: Exod. 7.10–12
Moses: the plagues of Egypt: Br
Text: Exod. 7.20–10.19
Moses: crosses the Red Sea: Ca, Mu, Hu, Br, Sg, Sa

Text: Exod. 14.19–29
Pharaoh: his army submerged in the Red Sea: Ca, Mu, Br, Sg, Sa
Text: Exod. 14.27,28
Moses: the Israelites pick up weapons of drowned Egyptians: Hu
Text: Apocryphal
Moses: praises the Lord for triumph over Pharaoh: Ca, Mu
Text: Exod. 15.1–19
Moses: receives the Tablets of the Law: Ca, Mu, Hu, Sg, Sa
Text: Exod. 31.18
Israelites worship the Golden Calf: Ca, Mu, Br, Sg
Text: Exod. 32.19
Moses: breaks the Tablets of the Law: Br
Text: Exod. 32.19
Moses: strikes down the Golden Calf: Hu
Text: Exod. 32.19
Moses: slaying of the worshippers of the Golden Calf: Mu
Text: Exod. 32.27,28
Moses: with Aaron in the Tabernacle: Ca, Mu
Text: Exod. 40.1–33
Moses: carrying of the Ark: Ca
Text: Num. 10.14–21
Moses: spies of Canaan return with grapes: Ca, Mu
Text: Num. 13.23–25
Moses: destruction of the men of Korah: Mu
Text: Num. 16.31–33
Aaron: offering incense and the rods of the tribes of Israel: Mu
Text: Num. 17.7,8
Moses: strikes the rock for water: Ca, Mu, Br, Sg, Sa
Text: Num. 20.11
Moses: the Brazen Serpent: Ca, Mu
Text: Num. 21.9

Balaam
Balaam: riding on the ass: Mu
Text: Num. 22.31

Phineas
Phineas: slays Zimri and Cozbi: Mu

Text: Num. 25.7, 8

Joshua
Joshua: the priests carrying the Ark: Mu
Text: Jos. 6.6–16
Joshua: the fall of Jericho: Ca, Mu, Hu
Text: Jos. 6.20–25
Joshua: stoning of Achan: Br
Text: Jos. 7.25
Joshua: capture of Hai: Br
Text: Jos. 8.1–29
Joshua: makes peace with the Gibeonites: Br
Text: Jos. 9.1–27
Joshua: hail descends on the attackers of Gibeon: Br
Text: Jos. 10.11

Jephthah
Jephthah: his daughter returns harping: Hu
Text: Jud. 11.34, 35
Jephthah: kills his daughter: Hu
Text: Jud. 11.39

Samson
Samson: with his parents: Ld
Text: Jud. 13.24
Samson: fighting the lion: Ld
Text: Jud. 14.6
Samson: carries off the gates of Gaza: Ld
Text: Jud. 16.3
Samson: destroys the Temple: Ld
Text: Jud. 16.25–30

Ruth
Elimelech and Naomi: Mu
Text: Ruth 1.1, 2
Elimelech's sons take Moabite wives: Mu
Text: Ruth 1.4
Tombs of Elimelech and his sons: Mu
Text: Ruth 1.5

Naomi with Ruth and Orpah: Mu
Text: Ruth 1.8–14
Ruth: brings grain to Naomi: Mu
Text: Ruth 2.18–22
Ruth: gleaning: Mu, Br
Text: Ruth 2.23
Ruth: at feet of Boaz: Mu, Br
Text: Ruth 3.7–13
Boaz: makes pact with kinsmen: Mu, Br
Text: Ruth 4.7–8
Boaz and Ruth: marriage: Mu
Text: Ruth 4.9–12
Boaz and Ruth: prayer for God's blessing on their marriage: Mu
Text: Ruth 4.11,12
Ruth: birth of Obed: Mu, Br
Text: Ruth 4.13–16
Boaz, Obed and Jesse: Mu
Text: Ruth 4.21,22

Samuel
Elkanah with Hannah and Peninnah: Mu, Hu
Text: 1 Kings 1.2
Hannah before Eli: Mu, Hu, Br
Text: 1 Kings 1.9–18
Samuel: birth: Mu, Hu, Br
Text: 1 Kings 1.20
Samuel: presented in the Temple: Mu, Hu, Br
Text: 1 Kings 1.24–28 or 1 Kings 2.20
Hophni and Phinehas: partaking of the meat from the sacrifice:
  Br
Text: 1 Kings 2.14
Samuel: anoints Saul: Ca, Mu, Hu
Text: 1 Kings 10.1
Samuel: speaks to Saul: Hu
Text: 1 Kings 15.1–3
Samuel: anoints David: Mu, Hu, Sg
Text: 1 Kings 16.13

David
David: offered armour by Saul: Ca

Text: 1 Kings 17.38, 39
David: fighting Goliath: Ca, Hu
Text: 1 Kings 17.48–50
David: beheading Goliath: Ca, Hu
Text: 1 Kings 17.51
David: brings Goliath's head to Saul: Ca
Text: 1 Kings 17.57
David: given the hallowed bread and the sword of Goliath: Mu
Text: 1 Kings 21.1–6
Saul: orders Doeg to slay the priests: Mu
Text: 1 Kings 22.17–19
Jonathan: death: Hu
Text: 1 Kings 31.2
Saul: death: Ca, Hu
Text: 1 Kings 31.4–6
David: anointed king: Ca
Text: 2 Kings 2.4
David: walks harping before the ark: Mu
Text: 2 Kings 6.14–16
David: his ambassadors shaved by the Ammonites: Mu
Text: 2 Kings 10.4
Absalom: hanging by hair from tree: Hu
Text: 2 Kings 18.9
Absalom: death: Hu
Text: 2 Kings 18.14
David: instructs Joab to number the people: Mu
Text: 2 Kings 24.1–3
Joab: numbers the people: Mu
Text: 2 Kings 24.4–8
David: told by Joab of the numbers: Mu
Text: 2 Kings 24.9
The men of Israel and Judah: Mu
Text: 2 Kings 24.9
David: laments his sin: Mu
Text: 2 Kings 24.10
David: spoken to by the prophet Gad: Mu
Text: 2 Kings 24.13, 14
Pestilence in Israel: Mu
Text: 2 Kings 24.15

Angel of the Lord commanded by God "It is enough": Mu
Text: 2 Kings 24.16
David: repents of his sin: Mu
Text: 2 Kings 24.17
David: instructed by the prophet Gad to build an altar: Mu
Text: 2 Kings 24.18
David: meeting with Araunah: Mu
Text: 2 Kings 24.20–22
David: sacrifice at the threshing floor of Araunah: Mu
Text: 2 Kings 24.25

Solomon
Solomon: judgment: Jo
Text: 3 Kings 3.16–27

Jeroboam
Jeroboam: prophecy of the birth of Josias and the destruction of
the altar of Jeroboam: Mu
Text: 3 Kings 13.1–5
Prophet of Bethel: the prophet of Juda at table and slain by a
lion: Mu
Text: 3 Kings 13.11–24

The Munich Psalter alone also contains scenes from the Lives
of Daniel, Susanna, Holofernes, Judith, Esther, and Jonah.

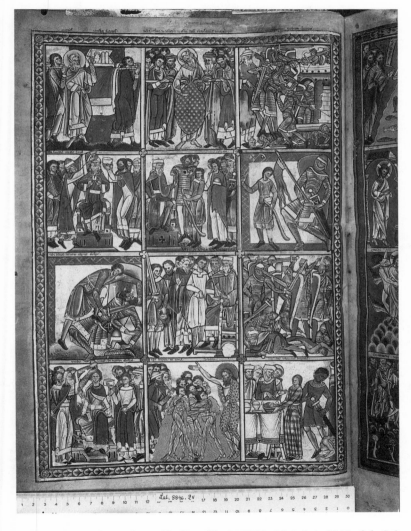

Fig. 1. Great Canterbury Psalter (Paris, Bibl. Nat. lat. 8846, fol. 2v). Moses, Joshua, Saul and David scenes.

Fig. 2. Single leaf from a Psalter (Cambridge, Fitzwilliam Mus. 330). Adam, Eve, Cain, Abel and Lamech scenes.

Fig. 3. Carrow Psalter (Baltimore, Walters Art Gall. W.34, fol 22v). Angel gives spade and spindle to Adam and Eve.

Fig. 4. Psalter (Cambridge, St. John's K.26, fol. 5). Angel comes to Adam and Eve in their labors.

Fig. 5. Bible Picture Book (Baltimore, Walters Art Gall. W. 106, fol 5.)
Third Plague of Egypt: the sciniphs.

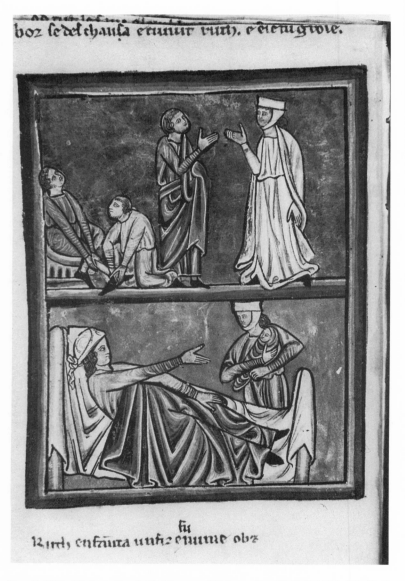

Fig. 6. Bible Picture Book (Baltimore, Walters Art. Gall. W.106, fol. 18v).
Boaz: pact with kinsmen; Birth of Obed.

Fig. 7. Munich Psalter (Munich, Bayerische Staatsbibl.Clm.835, fol. 13v).
Joseph sent to his brothers and sold to the Ishmaelites.

Fig. 8. Munich Psalter (Munich, Bayerische Staatsbibl.Clm.835, fol. 14).
Joseph sold to Potiphar and seduced by Potiphar's wife.

Fig. 9. Bible Picture Book (Baltimore, Walters Art Gall. W.106, fol. 15). Joseph accused by Potiphar's (Pharoah's) wife.

Fig. 10. Bible Picture Book (Baltimore, Walters Art Gall. W.106, fol. 16). Cup found in Benjamin's sack; Meeting of Jacob and Joseph.

Fig. 11. Psalter (Cambridge, Trinity Coll. B.11.4, fol. 10v). Joseph scenes.

Fig. 12. Psalter (Cambridge, Trinity Coll. B.11.4, fol. 7). Joseph scenes.

Fig. 13. Psalter (Cambridge, Trinity Coll. B.11.4, fol. 7v). Joseph scenes.

Fig. 14. Salisbury Chapter House (partly restored). Joseph seduced and accused by Potiphar's (Pharoah's) wife.

General Index

Aaron, 5, 83, 88, 179ff.
Abel, 24, 81, 82, 154–57, 175ff.
Abraham, 2, 31, 60, 61, 91, 154, 156–57, 159–60, 163, 176
Absalom, 32, 183ff.
Achan, 181ff.
Adam, 24–28, 38, 42, 151, 154–60, 166, 175ff.
Advent, Liturgy of, 100ff.
Aelfric, *Hexateuch*, 149, 167, 171
Aelred, St., 3
Aeneas, 26
Aeneid, 25, 66
Alexis, St., 7, 60–64, 66, 71, 74
Alighieri, Dante (*see* Dante)
Aliscans, 28
Ammonites, 170, 183ff.
Amos, 88, 91
Andreas Capellanus, 35
Angels, Rebel, 160, 174ff.
Anselm, St., 6, 7
Antichrist 42
Antiquitates Iudaicae, 165
Apocalypse, 8, 86, 96, 113–14, 122; Spanish MS, 105
apocrypha, 25, 81, 92, 103, 108, 115, 118, 126, 128, 130, 142, 146, 165–66, 168, 169, 173–75, 178, 180
Araunah, 184
Archipoeta, 35, 40, 41
Arme Heinrich, Der, 31
Arnaut, Daniel, 36
Art of Courtly Love, 35
Ashburnham Pentateuch, 81, 82, 95
Augustine, 20, 51, 60; Augustinian, 55, 58, 64, 73, 159; *De Doctrina Christiana*, 53–56, 57, 61; *Soliloquia*, 54; Augustinian nunnery, 159

Aurora, 152, 164

Babel, Tower of, 176ff.
Balaam, 5, 114, 162, 181ff.
Barbi, Michele, 37
Barabbas, 40, 46
Bede, 70
Being, 1, 2; identification of logos and being, 55
Benedictine, 109, 128, 157, 159; Benedictine nunnery, 159
Benjamin, 170, 178ff.
Bernard, St., 6
Bernard Silvestris, 66
Bible, 2, 3, 6, 9, 11, 15, 16, 19, 20, 23–28, 35, 36, 40–48, 51, 52, 54, 64, 65, 78, 81, 83, 84, 85, 87–93, 92–95, 97, 101, 102, 103, 109, 149, 151–54; *Bible des Sept Etats du Monde*, 165; *Bible historiale*, 165; *Bible moralisée*, 122, 135, 142, 147; Bible of Jehan Malkaraume, 165; Bible of William of Hales, 169; Bible picture books, 156–57; *Biblia pauperum*, 103; Bury Bible, 87, 91, 92, 95; Holkham Bible picture book, 172; Lambeth Bible, 77, 87, 88, 93–96, 101, 102; Lincoln Bible, 84, 91; Lothian Bible, 153, 154; Ripoll Bible, 86, 95; Roda Bible, 92, 95; Syriac Bible, 83, 91
Bible and Medieval Culture, The, 36
Boaz, 90, 170, 182ff.
Bonaventure, St., 1, 2, 12; *Collations*, 1, 13; Pseudo–Bonaventuran *Speculum vitae Christi*, 9, 11
Boniface VIII, 43, 48
Book of Vices and Virtues, The, 1
Brailes, William de, 149, 160, 163, 167

Index to Biblical Citations